*Phil Lee*



# 111 Places in Derby That You Shouldn't Miss

*Photographs by Rachel Ghent*

111

emons:

**Bibliographical information of the Deutsche Nationalbibliothek**
The Deutsche Nationalbibliothek lists this publication in the Deutsche Nationalbibliografie; detailed bibliographical data are available on the internet at http://dnb.d-nb.de.




Cäcilienstraße 48, 50667 Köln
info@emons-verlag.de

Layout: Editorial Design & Art Direction, Conny Laue, by Lübbeke | Naumann | Thoben
Maps: altancicek.design, www.altancicek.de
Basic cartographical information from Openstreetmap, © OpenStreetMap-Mitwirkende, OdbL
Edited by: Ros Horton
Printing and binding: sourc-e GmbH
Printed in Europe 2025
ISBN 978-3-7408-2432-7
First edition

*Guidebooks for Locals & Experienced Travellers*
Join us in uncovering new places around the world at
www.111places.com

# Foreword

The three big cities of the East Midlands – Derby, Nottingham and Leicester – often struggle to get themselves heard, but perhaps the mistake is to lump them all together in the first place. It's true they share one international airport, East Midlands, but even here there have been arguments about the airport's name, while the remit of the newly elected Mayor of the East Midlands does not even cover Leicester – which has its own mayor, thank you very much. And so we come to Derbyshire, one of England's most geographically diverse, fascinating and perhaps least understood counties, its northern reaches extending to the edge of both Manchester and Sheffield, while in the south it stretches as far as the townships that prefigure Birmingham.

The main magnet for visitors to Derbyshire is, of course, the Peak District, and every year millions enjoy its wild scenery, hiking over hill, dale, moor and mountain, but in the process many miss the more discrete attractions of Derby, one of the most interesting and underrated cities in England. It was here in Derby, beside the River Derwent, that what is usually considered to be the first factory in the world was opened and, for a few decades, the town was at the forefront of European thought and endeavour, its luminaries – Erasmus Darwin, Joseph Wright and so forth – key figures in the Enlightenment of the 18th century. Derby is dotted with reminders of those pioneering days and of the Victorian economic boom that followed, from grand industrial buildings and monuments through to parks, mills and bridges.

There's more. Within easy reach of Derby are grand country mansions such as Calke Abbey and Kedleston Hall, beguiling villages like Ticknall and Dale Abbey and the delightful town of Melbourne with its handsome hall and Norman church. Spend time in Derby and its environs and we bet you'll be surprised and enthralled.

# 111 Places

Royal School
for the Deaf Derby

# 1 27 Queen Street

*The Enlightenment rides high*

Running north from Derby cathedral, Queen Street is really rather humdrum, but here at no. 27 is one of the few buildings that take you back to the time when the town was at the very heart of the Enlightenment – hence the blue plaque. The house was built in the 1670s for the Flamsteed family, the most distinguished of whom was John Flamsteed (1646–1719), an astronomer of distinction, who spent years charting the stars, often using equipment he had invented himself.

Later, the clockmaker and scientist John Whitehurst (1713–1788) lived here. Whitehurst has several claims to fame, but is mainly remembered as the co-founder of Birmingham's Lunar Society in the 1760s. This group of inventors, intellectuals, and industrialists played a key role in the evolution of Enlightenment thinking – and they named their society after their habit of meeting during the full moon, when the extra light made the journey home easier and safer. Whitehurst was also a friend of no less a figure than Benjamin Franklin (1706–1790) and it seems likely that the American polymath and 'Founding Father' visited him in Derby during one of his extended stays in England. In the early 1780s, Franklin also had his portrait painted by Derby's Joseph Wright and – by happenstance – the same artist spent the last years of his life living here at Queen Street (plagued by his asthma).

Given all these historical resonances, it's really rather deplorable that the house is in such poor condition, though there are (vague) plans to refurbish the property. That said, the house isn't all that it seems: at first glance, the building appears to have the harmonious symmetries of the Queen Anne style, but in fact the façade dates from a 1920s rebuild, the result of a road widening scheme. Incidentally, the large exterior clock is a left-over from the days when Smith of Derby clockmakers was based here.

Address 27 Queen Street, Derby, DE1 3DS | Getting there A 13-minute walk from Derby bus station | Hours Exterior always viewable but no public access | Tip The mixed commercial block next door to 27 Queen Street is worth a second look for its 1930s Art Deco flourishes.

# 2 37 Cornmarket

*A goalscorer and a guardsman*

Busy and somewhat dishevelled, the Corn Market, in the centre of Derby, is flanked by commercial buildings of various dates and styles. Nonetheless, it's still a surprise to spy the Georgian façade and anachronistic tunnel-carriageway beside Subway at no. 37. Stroll down the tunnel and you soon reach Lock-Up Yard, a small, untidy space occupied for the most part by a seafood stall and leading into the Market Hall.

A short marble pillar in the Yard celebrates the life of Derby County's goalscoring ace Steve Bloomer (1874–1938), one of the few English strikers to be imprisoned by the Germans – football fans have often suggested others. Bloomer ran out of luck. He was working in Germany as a football coach when World War I broke out and he ended up being interned for the duration.

Also in Lock-Up Yard, set into the flagstones at the spot where the charging desk of the old police station once stood, is a memorial plaque honouring P. C. Joseph Moss (1853–1879). An ex-Grenadier Guard, Moss was murdered here in sensational events that grabbed national headlines. To begin with, there was a 'fallen' woman, Annie Green, and her drunken boyfriend, Gerald Mainwaring, roaming town in their horse and cart at breakneck speed; there was a chase; an arrest and then the couple were taken to the police station in Lock-Up Yard. Here, in a dramatic denouement, Annie fought with the police, which infuriated Mainwaring, who drew his revolver, declaring 'I will have no more of that' and promptly shot Moss.

Mainwaring would have been expecting execution, but at trial the jury could not decide between manslaughter and murder – and when news leaked out of some odd goings-on in the jury room, of coins being tossed and lots drawn, Mainwaring became the unlikely recipient of much public sympathy. In the event, he escaped the noose and got penal servitude instead.

Address 37 Corn Market, Derby, DE1 2DG | Getting there A 10-minute walk from Derby bus station | Hours Exterior always visible | Tip A couple of minutes' walk away from Lock-Up Yard, the Book Café (www.thebookcafe.co.uk), one of the city's better cafés, occupies a grand old neo-classical bank building at 21 Corn Market.

# 3 45 St Peter's Street

*A Boots to a Costa – and a fine-looking building*

Pedestrianised St Peter's Street, in the centre of Derby, may be a tad underwhelming, but it does possess several attractive buildings, the pick of which, at the junction with East Street, holds a Costa Coffee. It was actually Boots the Chemist who decided to open a shop here in the 1910s and they gave one of their favourite architects – Albert Nelson Bromley (1850–1934) – the commission. Bromley certainly wasn't fazed by the offer: over a lifetime, he did extremely well from Boots, dying a millionaire several times over.

At the time, Boots favoured a sort of neo-Tudor style and this is what Bromley provided, with fancy oriel windows framed and flanked by decorative plasterwork (pargetting) to the highest standard. To add a little extra lustre, Boots had four delicate miniature statues of local worthies added to the façade, each in its own niche – Florence Nightingale, John Lombe, Jedediah Strutt and the historian Will Hutton.

In the 1930s, the building was extended along East Street in a very similar but slightly plainer style. The extension is now a branch of the Halifax Building Society and it carries a blue plaque commemorating this as the birthplace of the pioneering meteorologist Sir George Clarke Simpson (1878–1965). Sir George did much to develop the science of weather forecasting both here and in India, but he is usually remembered as the meteorologist on Captain Scott's ill-fated dash to the South Pole.

A popular chap, known as 'Sunny Jim' on the Scott expedition, Simpson took his job seriously, building a prototype weather station and floating balloons in his attempt to predict the polar weather. Simpson returned from Antarctica in August 1912. At that time, he knew Scott had lost the race to the pole, but did not know of his ultimate fate; this he discovered in India. He is said to have been heartbroken.

Address 45 St Peter's Street, Derby, DE1 2AB | Getting there A 10-minute walk from Derby bus station | Hours Exterior always visible | Tip From Costa Coffee, it's just a short walk up the street to the handsome Victorian building that arches round the junction of St Peter's Street and Babington Lane. This is the Babington Buildings, which now accommodate Derby's excellent Waterstones bookshop, at 78–80 St Peter's Street.

# 4 Alan Bates Plaque

*Derby's finest actor?*

Surely one of the finest actors of his generation, Alan Bates (1934–2003) was born in Derby – and a blue plaque marks his childhood home, a pleasant detached house in Allestree, about three miles north of the city centre. Bates' first big break came when he won a scholarship to the Royal Academy of Dramatic Art (RADA) at a time when acting was beginning to de-gentrify (at least on the edges); his fellow students included Peter O'Toole and Albert Finney.

After RADA, Bates picked up a string of tasty roles in the theatre, but it was his outstanding performance as Cliff in John Osborne's *Look Back in Anger* that paved the way for his film career. This began in earnest in 1962 with *A Kind of Loving*, in which – at long last – a slice of working-class life hit the British screen courtesy of John Schlesinger and with Bates playing a restless, agitated protagonist, Vic Brown, who struggles to find contentment.

Bates' film career hit the heights in the late 1960s and 1970s when his sultry, husky, slightly hesitant charms worked a dream alongside Julie Christie in both *Far From the Madding Crowd* (1967) and *The Go-Between* (1971), a haunting, atmospheric film that is one of this author's favourites. In between these two was Ken Russell's riotous *Women in Love* (1969), in which – and this was a real shock at the time – Oliver Reed and Alan Bates wrestled together in the nude. Few if any actors could maintain these extraordinary cinematic feats and so it proved with Bates, but he continued working in TV, cinema and theatre for many years afterwards. He himself thought that his best performance was as the lead – Michael Henchard – in a 1978 TV version of Thomas Hardy's *The Mayor of Casterbridge* (1978).

Bates never shied away from his Derbyshire roots, rather the opposite, and after his death from pancreatic cancer, he was buried at All Saints' Church, in the Derbyshire village of Bradbourne.

**Address** Alan Bates birthplace, 3 Derwent Avenue, Allestree, Derby, DE22 2DP | **Getting there** A 10-minute drive north of Derby Market Place | **Hours** Private residence, always visible from the outside during daylight hours, but please be mindful of homeowner's privacy | **Tip** If mention of Bates' life and career has whetted your interest, you might want to read Donald Spoto's 2007 biography *Otherwise Engaged: The Life of Alan Bates*. Incidentally, the nude wrestling scene in *Women in Love* took place in Elvaston Castle.

# 5 Alexandra Hotel

*Trumpeting Castle Rock brewery*

The revival of British beer brewing over the last 30 years has been nothing short of miraculous, and Derbyshire has joined in the boozy bonanza, now boasting a hatful of small breweries. Rivalry between these breweries has sometimes been intense, but most would acknowledge their debt to Chris Holmes, who can claim to have kick-started the beer revival in the East Midlands, when he opened his own pub near Nottingham in 1977.

Holmes, who had been chair of CAMRA (the Campaign for Real Ale), knew what he was about and, flouting the monopolistic brewers of the day, he installed a row of hand pumps in his pub to dispense real ale. This proved to be a great success, and the company Holmes founded subsequently grew by leaps and bounds. Today, several of the best pubs in the East Midlands are owned and operated by his company, now called Castle Rock. All are committed to selling cask beers from a variety of brewers, though pride of place mostly goes to the beverages produced by the company itself – they started brewing their own beers in 1997. The brewers at Castle Rock have proved to be an inventive lot, but perhaps their greatest success is the award-winning blonde beer, Harvest Pale: at 3.8 per cent, this is described as having a 'delicate citrus character', and remains a real favourite. For something stronger, you might try the really very tasty, amber-coloured Preservation, at 4.4 per cent.

Most Castle Rock pubs are in Nottingham, but the company has ventured over to Derby, where the excellent Alexandra Hotel maintains the brewery's high standards, though this particular pub is tenanted rather than directly owned. Housed in a pleasant, three-storey Victorian building, the Alexandra is a traditional, beer-lovers' sort of place with bare wood floors and straightforward décor plus railway memorabilia in the lounge. It was also the birthplace of Derby CAMRA in 1974.

**Address** 203 Siddals Road, Derby, DE1 2QE, +44 (0)1332 293993, www.castlerockbrewery.co.uk/pubs/alexandra-hotel | **Getting there** A 5-minute walk from Derby railway station | **Hours** Sun–Thu noon–11pm, Fri noon–midnight, Sat 11am–midnight | **Tip** The delightful Brunswick Inn occupies attractive Victorian premises at the end of Railway Terrace, just a few strides from the Alexandra. A cosy, traditional boozer, the Brunswick offers a good range of real ales and is home to a micro-brewery.

# 6 Alice Wheeldon Plaque

*Uproar in Normanton*

On the south side of the city, in a modest house on Pear Tree Road, in Normanton, a celebrated criminal case gathered momentum in 1916. The case centred on Alice Wheeldon (1866–1919), who ran a second-hand clothes shop at number 12 – as recalled by today's blue plaque. A brave and resourceful woman, Alice was a feminist, a socialist and a suffragist, who vociferously opposed World War I at a time when war fever had gripped the nation. It was a dangerous set of beliefs for Alice to have, especially as her son, William, was hiding away as a conscription dodger.

Despite the risks, Alice established a network to help men who were avoiding military service. In late 1916, matters became more complicated when Alex Gordon and Herbert Booth turned up at her door seeking help as conscientious objectors. The two were, in fact, undercover agents working for MI5 and, in the way of such agents, Gordon was soon hamming it up, alleging that the Wheeldon family had concocted a conspiracy to murder Prime Minister Lloyd George by shooting him with poisoned darts.

On 31 January, 1917, Alice, two of her three daughters – Hettie and Winnie – and her son-in-law, Alfred Mason, were arrested and charged with conspiracy. Preposterous or not, the jury believed Booth's testimony, and Alice was sentenced to ten years, Alfred seven and Winnie five; Hettie, the third sister, was acquitted but died young – in 1920. Ominously, this was the first trial in English legal history to rely entirely on the evidence of a secret agent, and a campaign against the sentences soon began. In fairness to the British state, there was a feeling in government circles that the sentences were unjust and Lloyd George intervened to have Alice freed in 1918; Alfred and Winnie were released soon after. An elated Hettie announced that they were observing the 'convulsive death rattle of capitalism' – not, as it turned out, an accurate prophecy.

**Address** Mirpur Jewellers, 12 Pear Tree Road, Normanton, Derby, DE23 6PY | **Getting there** A 30-minute walk from Derby bus station; bus 38 from the bus station to the Vulcan stop | **Hours** Plaque visible during daylight hours | **Tip** The travails of Alice Wheeldon may well have been forgotten were it not for Nicola Rippon's *The Plot to Kill Lloyd George* and Sheila Rowbotham's *Friends of Alice Wheeldon*. Alice's son, William, fled to the Soviet Union, where his support for Trotsky cost him his life in 1937.

# 7 Alter Rock Climbing

*Up, up and away: indoor climbing and bouldering*

Right across the country, in towns and cities alike, there's a problem of just what to do with all those redundant churches now that congregations have shrunk so dramatically. It's a fairly recent phenomenon too – new mainstream churches were being built well into the 1960s – but the decline seems unstoppable and it's the sombre and surly Victorian churches that are often most at threat and in need of some luck to survive.

One of these lucky old churches is St James, in the Rose Hill neighbourhood, just a mile or so south of Derby railway station. Rose Hill was once a prosperous part of Derby and, in the 1860s, its well-heeled residents wanted a new church. They would also seem to have desired something out of the ordinary, as the London architect they commissioned, Joseph Peacock (1821–1893), specialised in designing churches that looked novel or just different from the norm. Sure enough, Peacock got to work and the new church, with its distinctive rough-stone exterior, was finished in 1867. It possessed a fairly standard nave, punctuated by neo-Gothic pointed windows, but the chancel was bold and ambitious – and looked distinctly French.

After deconsecration, St James was turned into the Alter Rock Indoor Climbing Centre in 2008. The centre now has over 6,500 square feet of graded, multi-coloured climbing walls and these can help prospective climbers ramp up their skills at whatever pace suits them best. Other enticing activities include a potential crawl through the Labyrinth Cave with a head torch to help you find your way and a swing along the Air Walk Aerial Obstacle Course. Alter also does bouldering – in which large and strategically positioned crash mats stand in for ropes. If you want to try your hand, but aren't sure, they run regular Tester Climbing Sessions. Incidentally, the climbing routes are regularly reset by experienced climbers.

**Address** St James Church, Malcolm Street, Derby, DE23 8LU, +44 (0)1332 367200, www.alter-rock.co.uk | **Getting there** A 30-minute walk from Derby bus station; bus 38 | **Hours** Mon, Tue, Thu & Fri 4–9pm, Wed 4–10pm, Sat 9am–4pm, Sun noon–4pm | **Tip** The Alter Rock Climbing Centre is a 10-minute walk from Pear Tree Plaza, where the former library has the most handsome of façades; it is now a small shopping centre. Here also is St Thomas, a second Joseph Peacock church.

# 8 Ashbourne

*A charming little town*

With a population of just 10,000, the small and lively town of Ashbourne, some 14 miles northwest of Derby, is a major gateway to the Peak District – so expect to see a surfeit of hiking boots. At the centre of things is the cobbled Market Place, a sloping triangular affair flanked by a particularly delightful medley of 18th- and 19th-century buildings, all cramped and squeezed together. The architectural highlight is the Town Hall, whose fancy Italianate façade of 1861 was designed by a Derby architect, the prolific Benjamin Wilson, who plumped for the Italianate style whenever he had half a chance. That said, it seems there was something about the cheek-by-jowl layout of the Market Place that rattled Ashbourne's gentry, who once complained that their fellow citizens were given over to 'idleness, drunkenness and whoredom'.

Footsteps from the Market Place, St John Street is spanned by an unusual, gallows-style advertising sign for the Green Man and Black's Head Royal Hotel. The sign dates from the time when Ashbourne was a major coaching stop, but it has recently been modified with the removal of the (controversial) black man's head that was perched on top.

Nearby is St Oswald's Church, whose mighty spire soars above a chunky nave and chancel of pink-tinted limestone. Inside, the church is a tad gloomy, but there's recompense in the magnificent stained glass with both the east and west windows the work of that Victorian stained glass specialist, Charles Kempe (1837–1907). It is, however, the Cockayne Chapel that grabs the attention, its platoon of exquisitely carved alabaster table tombs holding the earthly remains of the lords of the manor, the Cockaynes. Among them, perhaps the most exquisite is that of Sir John (d. 1477) and his wife, both with hands clasped in prayer, him in his armour, her in a splendid gown, her hair netted and braided.

**Address** St Oswald's Church, 5 School Lane, Ashbourne, DE6 1DN, +44 (0)303 3000498, www.ashbournechurch.org.uk | **Getting there** From Ashbourne, it's about 14 miles to Derby; there are regular buses between the two; Ashbourne bus station is on King Edward Street, a 5-minute walk from the Market Place | **Hours** St Oswald's Church: daily 10am–5pm | **Tip** Ashbourne has several great pubs and cafés, but one of the best is the Cornerstone, a neat and trim little place with a varied menu – mackerel pâté to falafel flatbread. It's near St Oswald's at the junction of Church Street and Station Road (www.bethskitchen.co.uk).

# 9 Ashby Castle

*From castle to fortified mansion*

Pocket-sized Ashby-de-la-Zouch, just inside Leicestershire, takes its fanciful name from two sources – the town's first Norman overlord was Alain de Parrhoet la Souche and the rest means 'place by the ash trees'. The ash trees may be long gone, but Ashby remains a pretty little market town and it holds one outstanding attraction, the substantial ruins of Ashby Castle, approached along a leafy little lane right in the town centre.

Originally a Norman manor house, the first castle here was the work of Edward IV's chancellor, Lord Hastings (1431–1483), who received his 'licence to crenellate' in 1474. But Hastings didn't enjoy his new home for long. Just nine years later, he was dragged from a Privy Council meeting to have his head hacked off on a log by order of the new king, Richard III (1452–1485). His crime was almost certainly his lacklustre support for the Yorkist cause, though Richard made the unlikely claim that Hastings had brought concealed weapons into the Privy Council in order to assassinate him.

The castle ruins include left-overs from various fortifications plus the shattered remains of the great hall, solar and chapel, but the star turn is the hundred-foot-high Hastings Tower, a self-contained four-storey stronghold that has survived in reasonably good nick. This tower house represented the latest thinking in castle design. It provided a secure inner fastness for Hastings and his retinue against both any outside enemy and his own mercenaries – who, experience had shown elsewhere, were often a threat to their employer; it also provided much better accommodation than was previously available. Improved living quarters reflecting the power and pride of the nobility were built all over England at this time and this is a rare survivor – witness the large windows on the upper floors, only accessible via the tower's well-worn spiral staircase.

Address South Street, Ashby-de-la-Zouch, Leicestershire, LE65 1BR, +44 (0)1530 413343, www.english-heritage.org.uk | Getting there Ashby is 12 miles south of Derby on the A511 (park in town centre car parks) | Hours Opening hours vary – see website | Tip From the Castle, it's just a few minutes' walk to the Loudon Memorial, a towering stone structure built to celebrate the life and times of a local aristocrat, Maud Hastings (1833–1874). It was one of Gilbert Scott's last designs and was based on the Eleanor Crosses raised by Edward I in the 13th century.

# 10 The Baseball Ground

*Did we really send men to fight in that?*

Among football fans of a certain vintage, mention of the Baseball Ground, the former home of Derby County Football Club, will almost certainly raise a smile. This is nothing to do with the quality of the football – D.C.F.C. have had periods of glut and famine like any other team – but on account of the mud. The Baseball Ground's playing area was below the level of the surrounding streets, which led to severe drainage problems with winter pitches effectively rolled mud and sand plus a few tufts of grass in the corners. The long-serving Derby groundsman, Bob Smith, who kept things afloat for 20 years (1964–1984), had no illusions, saying that when it rained it would be like putting 'water in a saucer of flour and it becoming gooey'.

Smith also claimed that Derby County's most illustrious manager, Brian Clough, who ruled the roost from 1967 to 1973, became fond of these quagmires, which he said suited his teams, though Clough may have had his tongue firmly in his cheek. Then, there was the famous penalty spot painting incident – which is now treasured on YouTube. On 30 April, 1977, the Derby player Archie Gemmill was scythed down and a penalty awarded. Clearly irritated, Joe Corrigan, the Manchester City goalie, then pointed out that there was no visible penalty spot – cue Bob Smith walking round the edge of the pitch, carrying a tape measure and a large pot of whitewash with a thick and stubby brush inside. Of course, this being the 1970s, Smith was wearing a jacket and tie as he would have thought appropriate for a representative of D.C.F.C.

In 1997, Derby County moved out to Pride Park, abandoning the Baseball Ground, which has since been redeveloped. The only reminder of past footballing glories now is *Football Stories* by Denis O'Connor, a charming and engaging steel sculpture of three silhouette footballers on a twisting platform.

Address *Football Stories* statue, Shaftesbury Crescent, Derby, DE23 8HG | Getting there A 10-minute drive south from Derby bus station | Hours Always accessible | Tip From Shaftesbury Crescent, it's a 15-minute walk south through suburban Derby to the tiny Pear Tree railway station, whose survival is something of a miracle. There are connections from here to Derby station.

# 11 The Bass Statue

*Three cheers*

A delicate, bronze effigy of Michael Thomas Bass (1799–1881), one of Derby's richest Victorians, stands tall on its pedestal in Museum Square, just off the Wardwick. Given the source of his fortune – the Bass family were brewers – the statue should really have Michael with a pint in hand, but not a bit of it: he is shown in serious, pensive mode, pondering over some document or other, dressed in his multi-buttoned waistcoat, bow tie and winged collar. The bronze is by the prolific Joseph Edgar Boehm (1834–1890), whose work pops up all over London.

Brewer he may have been, but this particular Bass was also a local philanthropist – he paid for Derby's old central library – and Member of Parliament, representing Derby from 1848 and 1883. A free trade, low tax Liberal, Bass kept a beady eye on those parliamentary nonconformists who opposed the sale of alcohol, but his political career was really rather undistinguished except, perhaps, for his somewhat eccentric attempts to rid the streets of barrel-organ grinders: quite what they had done to upset Bass is not clear.

Bass may have been an average politician, but he was a successful brewer. His father – also Michael Thomas (1760–1827) – had inherited the Bass brewery in Burton-on-Trent, just 12 miles from Derby, at a time when the Napoleonic Wars were threatening the brewery's bedrock trade with Russia. It was then that Bass Senr. spotted a new market – beer for British India, specifically 'India Pale Ale' in which a higher hop content than was customary acted as a natural preservative, preventing the ale from spoiling on the long voyage out. Bass Senr. made a fortune from the India trade as did Bass Jun., who took over the running of the company in 1827. Bass became the largest brewery in the world, producing 340,000 barrels in 1860, a million barrels by 1880, though the brewer's recent history has been problematic.

Address Museum Square, just off the Wardwick, Derby, DE1 1BS | Getting there A 12-minute walk from Derby bus station | Hours Always accessible | Tip Across the UK, a battalion of small brewers has usurped the likes of Bass – and Bass Charrington. In Derby, lookout for the brews of either the Shiny Brewery (www.shinybrewing.com) or the Derby Brewing Company (www.derbybrewing.co.uk).

# 12 Belper & Jedediah Strutt

*The Belper mills*

The twists and turns of the textile industry can be bafflingly complicated with hard-to-explain technological changes transforming things at a stroke. And so it is in the case of Jedediah Strutt (1726–1797), a Derbyshire farmer's son, who sold his horse to invest in a device that improved ribbed stockings. It worked a treat and so he patented the device, the Derby Rib machine, in 1759. This turned out to be the start of Strutt's stellar career, one that made him both wealthy and influential.

Strutt's energies were focused on the little town of Belper, where he opened his first cotton mill in 1776; 15 years later he had five mills in what had become a prodigious concentration of labour in a still rural Derbyshire. Jedediah's son and successor, William Strutt (1756–1830) was perhaps less welded to Belper, but just as successful, not least because of his interest in all things mechanical: he fiddled and improved his spinning mules and pioneered fire resistant, iron-framed buildings.

Belper's textile industry had more downs than ups after World War II, but it struggled on until, in the 1990s, the last outfit closed their factory in the East Mill, thereby adding to the pile of disused mills no one seemed to want.

Since then, some of the old mills have been demolished and others are slowly rusting away, gutters adrift, windows broken. Among the latter is the same East Mill, a vast structure, seven storeys high of red Accrington brick and with square corner towers. Completed in 1912, the East Mill dominates its immediate surroundings and lords it over the adjacent North Mill, the oldest and most architecturally important mill, a heavy-duty brick structure with cast-iron ceiling beams dating from 1804. The North Mill is yards from the River Derwent, where the gritstone weirs and walls were built to harness water power for the mills.

Address North Mill, Bridge Foot, Belper, DE56 1YD, www.belpernorthmill.org.uk | Getting there Belper is 10 miles north of Derby on the A38; hourly trains between the two; the North Mill is on the north side of Belper, a good 10-minute walk from the station – and 15 minutes from the Ritz Cinema | Hours Mar–Oct Wed, Sat & some Bank Holidays at 11am & 1.30pm for guided tours (see website for details) | Tip From the North Mill, it's the shortest of walks along the river to Belper River Gardens (daily 8am–dusk) with its immaculate flower beds and trim shrubberies.

# 13 Bennerley Viaduct

*The longest wrought-iron viaduct in England*

The Bennerley Viaduct is a supreme example of Victorian industrial architecture, its graceful trestle piers sweeping across the flood plain of the Erewash River 11 miles northeast of Derby. Opened in 1878, the viaduct was built for the Great Northern Railway (GNR), which was keen to muscle in on the lucrative business of transporting coal from the nearby mines.

At the time, viaducts were normally built of brick, but here the ground was subject to subsidence, so the architect-engineers opted for a much lighter structure with wrought-iron lattice work on both the bridge and its supporting piers, whose foundations were set on blue engineering bricks capped with stone. The end result is 1,452 feet long, with a maximum height of 60 feet – no wonder it was soon nicknamed 'The Iron Giant'. The engineers responsible were led by Richard Johnson (1827–1924). Johnson was an archetypal railway man, and an employee of GNR for many years, peppering the Midlands with his bridges while pushing the company to switch from iron to steel rails.

In 1968, Bennerley Viaduct was closed to rail traffic and left to its own devices, gradually disintegrating as time passed by, but dodging British Rail plans to have it demolished. Fortunately, this sad state of affairs attracted the attention of a band of volunteers, who were incorporated as the Friends of Bennerley Viaduct in 2015. Slowly but surely, the Friends have attracted enough funding to both repair the viaduct and provide access to the public. New polycarbonate decking means it's possible to walk from one end of the viaduct to the other with ramp access from the west and, before the end of 2025, from the east too. A visitor centre and a café are also promised. The best viewing points are on the east side, and the viaduct links in with the 30-mile Erewash Valley Trail, a popular cycling and walking route.

**Address** Bennerley Viaduct Visitor Centre, Shilo Way, Awsworth, Nottingham, NG16 2BF, www.bennerleyviaduct.org.uk | **Getting there** To get to the west end, take the train to Ilkeston, then it's a 25-minute walk along the Erewash Valley Trail. To get to the east end by car, take the A6096 Shilo Way from Derby to the Visitor Centre car park. Alternatively, take the A6096 to the Newton's Lane car park, Awsworth, and it's a pleasant 15-minute walk along the towpath beside the (disused) Nottingham canal. | **Hours** For opening hours, events and guided tours, check the website | **Tip** The Erewash Valley Trail is a circular, 18.5-mile long walking and cycling route running past the small industrial towns along the Nottinghamshire/Derbyshire border. The best known of these is Eastwood, where the novelist D. H. Lawrence (1885–1930) was born.

# 14 Bess of Hardwick Monument

*A stylish interment*

Born in relatively humble circumstances in Derbyshire, Bess of Hardwick (1527–1608) rose to become one of the most influential women in Elizabethan England. A Lady of the Queen's Bedchamber, Bess' wealth became legendary, and although much of it was secured via well-made marriages – she had four husbands – she was undoubtedly a shrewd businesswoman in her own right. Her fourth marriage, in 1568, was to one of the most powerful men in the land, George Talbot, the Earl of Shrewsbury, but in this case prominence carried a penalty: Queen Elizabeth obliged the couple to hold Mary, Queen of Scots, under what amounted to house arrest for 15 years. Even worse, as far as Bess was concerned, the queen shifted the costs of the imprisonment to the Shrewsburys, while Mary did her malevolent best to stir discord between the couple.

Bess' marriage was effectively over years before the earl died in 1590, but she put the matter firmly behind her with the construction of Hardwick Hall, one of the region's most magnificent mansions. Neither was she inclined to let the vagaries of fate decide her funerary monument – she had it constructed during her lifetime in Derby's church of All Saints, closely supervising the work of the man she put in charge, Robert Smythson, also the main architect of Hardwick Hall.

There things might have stayed, except that All Saints was demolished in the 1720s and Bess' monument had to be transferred to the replacement church. Perhaps surprisingly, it survived the move and today it stands on the right-hand side of the nave. A fancily carved affair, it is topped by a coat of arms between matching obelisks while Bess herself is down below, a recumbent alabaster figure of surprising crudity; above her is a laudatory plaque recounting her glories – all in Latin.

**Address** Derby Cathedral, 18–19 Iron Gate, Derby, DE1 3GP, +44 (0)1332 341201, www.derbycathedral.org | **Getting there** A 10-minute walk from Derby bus station | **Hours** Mon, Tue & Thu 8.30am–6.30pm, Wed 8.30am–6pm, Fri 8.30am–5pm, Sat 9am–5pm, Sun 8.30am–6.15pm | **Tip** If you're strolling down towards the River Derwent from the Cathedral, use Amen Alley, a lovely little lane on the south side of the church.

# 15 Birds Bakery

*Pork pies galore*

To discover the gastronomic tastes of the average East Midlander, head straight for Birds, whose neat and modern shops can be found dotted across the region with three in Derby. Still a family concern, Birds was founded in Derby in 1919 by three brothers, Frank, Thomas and Reginald. In 1951, it was passed on to two more Birds – another Reginald and Paul – who declared their ambition with refreshing simplicity: 'To provide our customers with the highest possible quality of cakes, pork pies, bread and savouries, at a reasonable cost and with a friendly and reliable service.' This proved a winning formula – and there are now over 60 outlets in total from Matlock in the north to Tamworth in the south.

Birds offers a variety of popular sweet and savoury treats. You can choose a chunky sausage roll, a freshly made-up roll (or 'cob' in the local dialect), a delicious mini-quiche or shiny teacake. Even more traditional are the tiny dishes of potted meat – sometimes called 'potted dog' hereabouts – and that's before you get to the oh-so-sugary cakes. These range from trifles to custard tarts, cream and jam doughnuts, cream slices and puffs through to delicious apple pies – this author's favourite since they stopped making their tastebud-exploding blackcurrant pies.

Most Birds shops also sell 'elephant's feet' – not, thank goodness, anything to do with the animal, but a choux pastry bun filled with whipped cream and topped with chocolate that does resemble, if rather vaguely, the aforesaid feet. Then there's a perennial favourite across the East Midlands, the pork pie, which consists of a compressed ball of meat encased in thick pastry. The traditional repast of the fox-hunting fraternity, the pork pie's popularity has spread far and wide, but it is something of an acquired taste, especially the jelly that fills the gap between the meat and the pastry.

**Address** In Derby, the most central Birds is at 20 Albert Street, Derby, DE1 2DS, +44 (0)1332 363770, www.birdsbakery.com | **Getting there** Albert Street is a 10-minute walk from Derby bus station | **Hours** Mon–Sat 8am–5pm | **Tip** All of the larger Birds outlets – including the one on Albert Street – take pre-orders for party food from cakes and croissants to pork pies and quiches.

# 16 Bonnie Prince Charlie

*Here today, gone tomorrow: a Jacobite surprise*

A conspicuous equestrian statue of Bonnie Prince Charlie – more properly Charles Edward Stuart (1720–1788) – stands at the heart of Derby, on Cathedral Green. It recalls the Prince's accidental, albeit crucial, stay here during the Jacobite Rebellion of 1745. In August of that year, the Prince had landed in Scotland, where he launched a rebellion aimed at putting the Stuarts back on the throne in place of the Hanoverian King George II. The Prince raised a Scottish Highland army of several thousand easily enough and marched south into England, but by the time he reached Derby, on Wednesday 4 December, 1745, his supply lines were sorely stretched and three Hanoverian armies were manoeuvring against him.

Despite the odds, Charles was keen to press on to London, convinced that he could capture the capital, but his commanders believed there was no hope of success, and insisted they retreat north. After several heated debates, Charles caved in – but, in what remains one of the UK's greatest counterfactuals, perhaps he was right: neither Charles nor his generals knew of the panic that had spread across London after news came that the Jacobites had reached Derby. In the event, the long and dispiriting withdrawal north ended with the destruction of the Highland army at Culloden.

In the early 1990s, the City Council finally decided to commemorate these dramatic events with a statue by the prolific Derbyshire-born sculptor Anthony Stones (1934–2016). Stones depicts the mounted Prince looking suitably determined as he gazes out into the middle distance, his slender frame kitted out in full bonnet, frock coat and riding boots. This romantic version of the Prince may well reflect something of his appearance when he arrived in Derby, but it does put a gloss on a man whose dynastic ambitions cost thousands of lives.

**Address** Cathedral Green, Derby, DE1 3AF | **Getting there** An 8-minute walk from Derby bus station | **Hours** Always accessible | **Tip** Bonnie Prince Charlie stayed for two nights in Derby at one of the town's largest mansions – Exeter House. This was demolished long ago, but some of its wood panelling was saved and has ended up in the Derby Museum & Art Gallery.

# 17 Breedon on the Hill

*Byzantines in Breedon? Surely not...*

The ancient church of St Mary and St Hardulph is glued to the top of a heavily quarried hunk of rock at Breedon on the Hill, a modest little village just beyond the Derbyshire border. This was the site of a prehistoric hillfort, whose scant remains lie on the west side of the hill, and then it was over to the kings of Mercia, who recognised Breedon's strategic importance by dispatching a band of monks to establish a priory here in the 7th century. The priory has disappeared in the mists of time, but the church you see today – a sturdy medieval structure with a chunky tower – has an especially intriguing interior.

To begin with, flanking the nave, there's the extravagant Shirley pew, a cage-like room within a room named after the family who bought the priory during the Reformation, and now inhabited by a trio of finely carved, 17th-century alabaster tombs. The grandest of these is a double decker, with a skeleton below and the Shirleys at prayer up above. Also edging the nave is an immaculately maintained Georgian box pew, but this is not nearly as rare as the Anglo-Saxon carvings scattered along the south side of the nave. Quite how they survived the turbulence of the Reformation is hard to say, but there are carvings of individual saints and angels, as well as wall friezes, where a dense foliage of vines encloses a tangle of animals and humans. Some of the figures, most memorably Mary and the saints positioned above the south-aisle altar, have drilled eyes into which were inserted precious stones; in the candle-lit interior of the Mercian priory this must have had a dramatic effect.

Remarkably, the figures don't look Anglo-Saxon at all – witness Mary's three-fingered salutation with the fourth finger touching her thumb, a classic Byzantine pose; who the sculptors were and how they came to be here at this remote spot has fuelled much academic debate. Art historian Nikolaus Pevsner said the sculptures were 'inexplicable'.

Address Breedon on the Hill, Derby, DE73 8AP, www.breedonpriorychurch.org | Getting there By car, it's a 16-mile drive south from central Derby to Breedon on the Hill. The village of Breedon on the Hill is at the foot of the hill, the church is at the top; the most obvious way to travel between the two is along the narrow, gated and winding half-mile lane that begins in the village at The Green – just follow the signs. You can walk up the lane at any time, but cars can only use the lane during the daytime. | Hours Daily Nov–Mar 9.30am–3.30pm; Apr–Oct 9.30am–7pm | Tip If you are walking to and from the church, you will be grateful for a drink – and the antique Holly Bush (www.hollybushbreedon.co.uk), in the village at the start of the route, will do very nicely.

# 18 Calke Abbey

*The decline of the gentry*

The grand façade of Calke Abbey house is all self-confidence, its acres of dressed stone and glass polished off with an imposing Greek Revival portico that was added in the early years of the 19th century. This all cost bags of money and the Harpurs and then the Harpur-Crewes, who owned the estate, were doing very well until the economics of the English country estate changed after World War I. Then, at a time when country houses were being demolished by the dozen, the Harpur-Crewes simply hung on, becoming the epitome of faded gentility and refusing to make all but the smallest of changes to the house – though they did finally plump for electricity in 1962.

The last Harpur-Crewe to live here, Charles, died in 1981 and the estate passed in its entirety to the National Trust. Much to their credit, the Trust decided not to bring in the restorers and have kept the house in its semi-dishevelled state ever since – and this, along with its splendid rural setting, is its real charm.

A visit usually starts in one of the old agricultural outbuildings, from where it's a short stroll to the house, whose Entrance Hall sets the scene, its walls decorated with ancient stuffed heads from the family's herd of prize cattle. Beyond is the Caricature Room, whose walls are lined with satirical cartoons, some of which were executed by the leading cartoonists of their day, including Gillray and Cruikshank. Further on, there are more animal heads and glass cabinets of stuffed birds in the capacious Saloon; an intensely cluttered Drawing Room; a Museum Room, which explores the life and times of Alice Pearse, the family's nurserymaid and nanny; and, oddly, a state bed given to the Harpurs by the daughter of George II in 1734 and then left unpacked until the National Trust arrived. After the house, you can wander out into the gardens, stroll the surrounding parkland and pop into the Victorian estate church.

Address Calke Abbey, Ticknall, Derby, DE73 7JF, +44 (0)1332 863822, www.nationaltrust.org.uk | Getting there Calke Abbey is a 15-mile drive south from Derby on the A514; from Derby bus station, take Arriva (Route 2) and alight at Ticknall (Calke Abbey Entrance), from where it's a 1.5 mile walk through the park. | Hours House and estate opening hours vary – see website | Tip Calke Abbey has a cut-above-the-average café and restaurant, which is located in the former stable yards, together with a second-hand bookshop.

# 19_Crich Tramway Village

*Tram heaven*

For the tram spotter and enthusiast alike, the Crich Tramway Village – aka the National Tramway Museum – is quite simply an El Dorado. Here, in this rural location, about 15 miles north of Derby, generations of volunteers have created a sort of tourist village surrounding the main focus of attention – the vintage trams that clank along a mile-long stretch of line. The trams are of various types and from various parts of the world and each is meticulously serviced and repaired. The line has five hop-on, hop-off stops for passengers, and costumed conductors ring their bells with all the enthusiasm you would hope for.

Trams are older than you might think – the first horse-drawn versions appeared in 1804 – but these were superseded by electric-powered trams in the late 19th century. Electric trams were themselves in steep decline by the 1940s and it was then that a group of tram *aficionados* had the idea of a tram museum to help conserve what they loved. Eventually, in the late 1950s, they happened upon a disused limestone quarry here at Crich, a fairly remote spot to be sure but one with the immediate advantage of its own mineral railway, designed by no less a figure than George Stephenson.

Since the purchase of the quarry, volunteers have assembled an international collection of trams along with the necessary tramway equipment. A sweet shop, pubs, cafés and gift shops have also been added, not to mention a couple of exhibition areas and – rather idiosyncratically – the façade of the old Derby Assembly Rooms. A particular highlight is the workshop viewing gallery, where you can watch the restorers and repairers on the job in the tram depots. Crich is a work in progress – a lot has been done and there's more to do – but it's a popular family day out and not the scene of slaughter as depicted in Ben Wheatley's tongue-in-cheek film *Sightseers*.

**Address** The National Tramway Museum, Crich, near Matlock, DE4 5DP, www.tramway.co.uk | **Getting there** Crich is 15 miles from Derby, 8 miles from junction 28 of the M1 | **Hours** Opening hours vary with the seasons, so check www.tramway.co.uk | **Tip** From the Tramway Museum, it's a short walk to the Crich Memorial Tower, a lighthouse-like, 1920s war memorial perched on a hill overlooking the Crich quarry. There's a tea-room here and memorial gardens. For opening times, go to www.mercianregiment.co.uk/crich.

# 20 Cromford Mill

*A world first – welcome to the cotton mill*

Seemingly tucked away from prying eyes, Cromford Mill is one of the region's most striking attractions, with a set of large and really rather stately stone buildings arranged around a central courtyard. Holy ground for the industrial archaeologist, this was where, in 1771, Richard Arkwright (1732–1792) founded the first water-powered cotton spinning mill. It was Arkwright's invention of the water frame – a spinning frame powered by a waterwheel – that made it all possible, along with cash from Jedediah Strutt. The frame meant that the spinning of the yarn from raw cotton could begin in earnest provided, that is, there was a continuous water supply – hence Cromford, where Arkwright could rely on a mixture of fresh water from the Bonsall Brook and warm water from the Cromford Sough, which drained the nearby lead mines.

Not a man to hang around, Arkwright started with 200 workers, mostly women and children, the youngest being just seven years old. Later, the minimum age was raised to ten. They worked two twelve-hour shifts, six days a week and the gate to Cromford Mill was shut at 6am and 6pm; any worker who arrived late was barred from working the rest of the day and was fined a day's pay too. These terms may seem outlandish today – and some thought so then – but few mill owners of that period were any more generous and Arkwright did provide limited sick pay and (some) housing.

Considering the historical importance of the mill, it seems bizarre that it was left to go to ruin for so long, but in recent years it's been skilfully restored with shops, a café and information boards explaining what happened where and why. Particular highlights include the 1796 mill manager's house just outside the main gate; the courtyard's watercourse and weir; and 'The Arkwright Experience', a lively and well-composed exhibition on the man's life and times.

Address Mill Road, Cromford, Matlock, DE4 3RQ, +44 (0)1629 823256, www.cromfordmills.org.uk | Getting there Cromford Mill is 20 miles north of Derby; train to Cromford's extremely picturesque station, then an easy 10-minute walk | Hours Mill courtyard open daily 9am–5pm; to visit the Arkwright Experience, start at the Visitor Centre, where you can book a guided tour | Tip From Cromford Mill, it's a 10-minute walk to the centre of Cromford, where Scarthin Books (www.scarthinbooks.com) is something of a local institution, noted for its relaxed atmosphere, vegetarian food and new and second-hand books.

# 21 Dale Abbey

*A lovely little village*

It's hard to think of a more beguiling hamlet than Dale Abbey, whose inordinately pretty main street – lined with handsome old cottages – slips down from the A6096 just seven miles east of Derby. As its name suggests, this was once the site of an abbey, a medieval foundation whose chief surviving fragment is the soaring stone arch left from the east window; conspicuous, it's just a couple of minutes' walk off the main drag. The abbey was suppressed without much fuss during the Dissolution of the Monasteries in the 1530s.

Nearby, up a gravel track at the end of the main street, is All Saints' Church, where, in a most unusual arrangement, the church is under the same roof as an attractive half-timbered house. The house started as the abbey infirmary before becoming The Bluebell Inn, with a connecting door said locally to lead from salvation to damnation; the door is gone and the house is now part of a farm. As for the church interior, it's a homely jumble with a 17th-century pulpit, a tangle of pews and box pews and an ancient wooden gallery. On the north wall is a restored medieval wall painting of the Visitation, a Biblical story that has a pregnant Virgin Mary visiting Elizabeth, who was herself pregnant with John the Baptist. The scene would have been familiar to the congregation and there is a warm tenderness in the women's embrace that is a joy to behold – even if most of the painting has worn away.

From the church, it's a 10-minute walk up steps and into the woods to reach the Hermit's Cave – or Hermitage – where a 12th-century Derby baker withdrew from the world after the Virgin Mary came to visit him in a dream. Carved into the sandstone cliffs above the village, the Hermitage is interesting in itself, though it's a shame it's not in better condition. Round off your visit with a cup of tea and a scone or sandwich at the charming Friars House Tearoom.

**Address** All Saints' Church, The Village, Dale Abbey, Ilkeston, DE7 4PN, +44 (0)115 9440609, www.sdrchurches.org.uk | **Getting there** Dale Abbey is about 7 miles from Derby off the A6096 | **Hours** Church hours vary – see website for further details; opening hours for the Friars House Tearoom also vary – take pot luck or call ahead (+44 (0)115 930 9152) | **Tip** From Dale Abbey, it's about a mile east to Windmill Farm, an attractively restored late 18th-century windmill with a popular café; it's on Cat and Fiddle Lane, Ilkeston, DE7 6HD, +44 (0)1332 955163.

# 22 Darley Abbey Mills

*Cotton mills galore*

It may have been swallowed up by Derby in the 1960s, but Darley Abbey, just a mile or so up along the River Derwent from the city centre, has a distinct and curious history, starting out – as indeed its name would suggest – as an abbey, though not a very successful one: finances became so stretched in the 14th century that several of the monks were given free transfers. Some locals blamed the incompetence of the abbots, but whatever the truth, the abbey did not outlast the Dissolution and the only surviving building, now the Abbey Inn, is a heavily buttressed, two-storey stone structure on the west side of the river, on Darley Street.

In the late 18th century, Darley Abbey's riverside location caught the eye of Thomas Evans (1723–1814), whose family had already made a fortune from Derbyshire lead mining. Evans purchased land on the east bank and this was where he built his Long Mill, the first of what were to be five, co-joined cotton spinning mills; the last mill wasn't finished until 1835 when the workforce peaked at just over 500. The Darley Abbey Mills closed in the late 1960s, leaving the city saddled with yet another platoon of potentially unwanted industrial buildings. Fortunately, they weren't bulldozed, largely because of their historical significance: comparatively few mills remain from the early years of industrialisation (say 1780 to 1840) and these also possess certain unique, albeit rather technical features, like an early fireproofing system.

Today, Darley Abbey Mills still feels like an industrial village and as you wander its lanes and alleys, you'll see old cotton mills and ancillary structures on every side. Light industry is here in these recycled buildings, but the emphasis now is more on restaurants and bars. Some parts of the complex are neat and trim, others less so, but the footbridge over the river certainly needs repair.

Address Haslams Lane, Darley Abbey, Derby, DE22 1DZ, www.darleyabbeymills.com | Getting there Darley Abbey Mills is 2 miles north of Derby bus station; the Comet Bus links the two | Hours Opening hours vary with the establishment, but the location itself is always accessible | Tip Darley's Restaurant & Terrace, Waterfront, Darley Abbey Mill, Derby, DE22 1DZ (www.darleys.com), is generally reckoned to be one of Derby's best restaurants. The menu is a canny combination of British and European dishes.

# 23 Darley Park

*A splendid park – and magnificent hydrangeas*

One of Derby's charms is the band of greenery that stretches north from the city centre along the banks of the River Derwent: few English cities have such a large slab of undeveloped land so close to the centre, though first-time visitors can find the layout a tad confusing. This whole strip of parkland is sometimes called 'Darley Park', but it actually comprises several adjacent urban parks. These begin in the south with Derwent Park on one bank and Parker's Piece on the other before continuing with Strutts Park and Darley Park. Taken together, these parks serve as the gateway to the 15-mile-long Derwent Valley Mills World Heritage Site, the apple of the local tourist industry's eye: the UNESCO award recognised that the modern factory/mill system started here in the 18th century.

The Evans family, who owned the Darley Abbey Mills, moved into Darley Hall, in the heart of what is now Darley Park, in 1835. Short of neither cash nor leisure, they added flower beds and shrubberies and landscaped the grounds, which perform a great sweep down a steepish slope to the River Derwent. Derby Council took possession of the estate in the 1930s and the hall was demolished as unsafe in 1962, but the old entrance, on Darley Park Drive, has kept its stone wall, ornate gates and porter's lodge.

Inside the park, among much else, are walking trails, a wildlife garden, a playground, a tearoom, a wildflower meadow and, perhaps the cream of the crop, the National Hydrangea Collection. This is the largest collection of hydrangeas in the UK, comprising some 400 different types, and it's supported by a band of dedicated volunteers, who plant and maintain it. Darley Park is also crossed by the Derwent Valley Heritage Trail, which links Derby railway station, the Museum of Making, Darley Abbey Mills and points north to Matlock and beyond.

**Address** Darley Park Drive, Darley Park, Derby, DE22 1EN www.inderby.org.uk | **Getting there** From Darley Park Drive, it's a 2-mile drive south to the city centre; bus to Darley Park Drive from Derby station | **Hours** Daily summer 9am–5pm; winter 9.30am–4.30pm, though parts of the garden vary their times – see the website for the latest information | **Tip** The streets of tiny Darley Abbey adjoining Darley Park are dotted with old terraced houses, many of which were built specifically for the mill hands: Brick Row has housing from the 1790s, Poplar Row the 1820s.

# 24 Denby Pottery Village

*Premium, locally made pottery*

The hamlet of Denby, nine miles south of Derby, sits near deposits of ironstone, coal and clay, three materials that pretty much defined the local economy for decades. The coal and the ironstone are no longer sought after, but Denby Pottery still uses the clay and is now the largest employer here. The origins of the company are somewhat convoluted – and read rather like a Jane Austen novel: a certain Robert Lowe of Locko Park died in 1785 leaving his estate to his daughter, Anne, on condition she married a man from a list of eligible bachelors he had provided. Anne was having none of this and, after legal action, settled for a wodge of money with the estate passing to Robert's cousin, William Drury-Lowe (1753–1827).

No slouch, William was an enterprising man, who must have been delighted when, in 1806, a wide seam of high-quality clay was found on his estate during the construction of a new road. William allowed a pottery factory on his land and this began to bloom and blossom under the Bourne family, who would, remarkably enough, remain in control until 1970. Salt-glazed, stoneware bottles were the mainstay of the pottery in its early days: glass was very expensive so these bottles were used for all and sundry – from ink to ginger beer.

In recent years, Denby Pottery has had a bumpy ride with frequent changes of ownership and management buy-outs, but full credit is due to them for the creation of Denby Pottery Village, a neat and trim complex in mostly modern buildings near what was once Denby Colliery. As you would expect, the shops here sell the full range of Denby products, often, but not exclusively, stoneware and mostly with substantial discounts. There are the usual leisure facilities also, including a garden shop and café. A separate block holds the Denby Museum and factory, where you can immerse yourself fully in this working pottery.

**Address** Denby Pottery Village, Derby Road, Ripley, DE5 8NX, +44 (0)1773 740799, www.denbypottery.com | **Getting there** Denby Pottery Village is about 8 miles north of Derby on the B6179; bus 9.3 to the Denby Visitor Centre | **Hours** Mon–Sat 9am–5pm, Sun 10am–4pm; pre-booking essential for Museum and Pottery Tour | **Tip** Next to the car park at the Denby Pottery Village is the winding wheel of Denby Hall Colliery, where coal was mined from 1877 to 1967. Close by was Denby Drury Lowe Colliery (1839–1968). They both produced top-quality coal that was much in demand as a household fuel, especially in London, where it was known as Derby Brights.

# 25 The Derbados Palm Tree

*High farce on the Derby ring road*

There's no general agreement as to where the East Midlands begins and ends – is Northamptonshire included, never mind Lincoln? – but local rivalries, say between Nottingham and Derby, are more exaggerated hereabouts than real, and everywhere there is a certain deadpan refusal to blow the regional trumpet.

Welcome, then, to the Derbados Palm Tree, the inconsequential palm tree that grows in the central reservation of the Derby ring road just to the north of the city centre – not far from the River Derwent. Under the tongue-in-cheek cry of 'Making Derby a slightly more interesting place to live', internet pranksters claimed the tree as an historic monument – in fact, the most interesting sight in the city. Like-minded reviewers rallied to the cause: 'What a welcome [sight] when coming back from outside the county,' opined one. 'As we approached the Derbados Palm Tree we were met with supportive horns and jeers from the other cars,' said another.

Faced with such obvious silliness – but realising the palm tree was passed by thousands of motorists every day – Derby City Council played it straight, commenting 'We're stumped as to why this tree is getting this attention. It may be unusual, but its location means it can't be safely viewed, so we'd question how many people have actually managed to see it.' Quite so.

Neither is this the first outing for 'Derbados', a singularly daft but really rather endearing merging of Derby and Barbados coined, it is assumed, as an effort to raise morale – or at least have some fun – in the depths of a gloomy Derby winter. It's hard to know where and when 'Derbados' was first used, though a spirited local newspaper article dated to 2014 did suggest 'If you don't like living in Derbados, why not just leave?' Since then, it has been popularised and is now used for all sorts from bike rides to designer T-shirts and hoodies.

Address The Upas, Derby, DE1 2ER | Getting there There's no access to the palm tree on foot, but if you do drive past it – it's on the dividing barrier between lanes of the A601 | Hours Always visible in daylight hours | Tip Derby's looping, outer ring road can seem inordinately long winded – but do not fear, escape is always at hand. You could, for example, turn north to let off some steam at Rollerworld Derby, Mansfield Road, Derby, DE21 4AW (www.derbyrollerworld.co.uk).

# 26 Derby Arboretum

*A very influential park*

Set among the Victorian terraces of Rose Hill, about a mile south of the Market Place, is the Derby Arboretum, whose manicured lawns and mature trees provide a welcome slice of greenery in this part of the city. The Arboretum lays claim to be England's first public park and although this is a matter of some debate, it was certainly one of the first when it opened in 1840.

The man who funded it was Derby's Joseph Strutt (1765–1844), whose family made a fortune from textiles. Strutt was a man with a mission. He believed in the power of art and culture to edify, even opening his own house to display his art works to Derby's untutored and tutored alike. Warming to his theme, Strutt decided to create a public park for the benefit of all and, to this end, he hired a Scottish landscape gardener by the name of John Claudius Loudon (1783–1843). A rare sort of man, Loudon had, by the time he met Strutt, cured himself of an opium habit, written *An Encyclopædia of Gardening* and survived a crude amputation of his right arm. In Derby, Loudon laid out Strutt's arboretum with gentle promenades and perimeter paths. Artificial mounds enhanced the landscape, trees were distributed artfully and an ironwork fountain pivoted one axis, a copy of the Uffizi (or Florentine) boar another. Curiously, the original boar had been admired by Strutt in Italy, so he had an earthenware copy made when he returned home; this was accidentally decapitated long ago and the present version is bronze.

In 1853, after both Strutt and Loudon had died, the final touches were added to the park: Arboretum Square became the main approach, flanked by comfortable Victorian houses and culminating in a fancy, Italianate façade with the figure of Strutt in the centre. Incidentally, one early visitor, who was almost certainly influenced by what he saw, was Frederick Olmsted, of New York's Central Park fame.

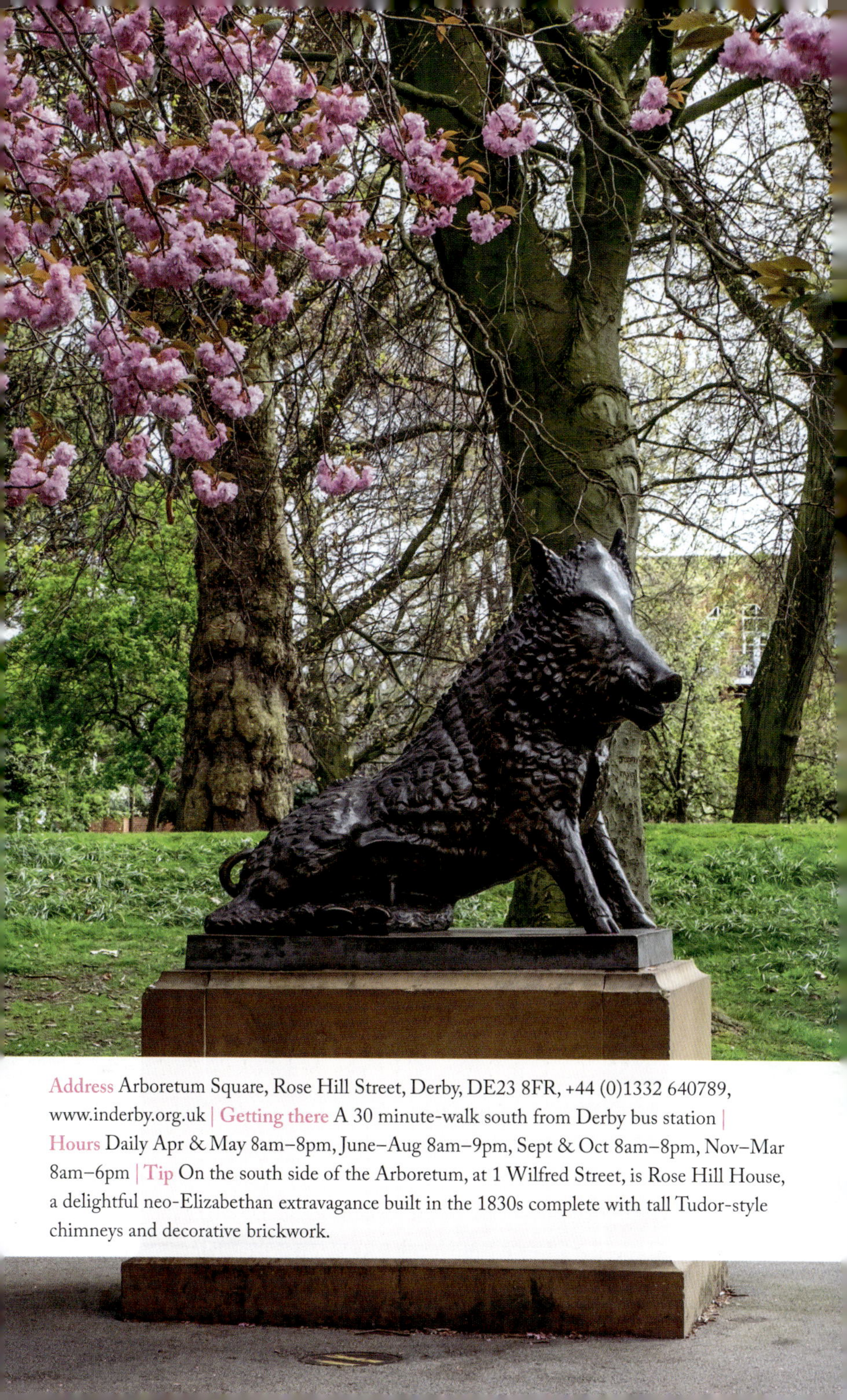

Address Arboretum Square, Rose Hill Street, Derby, DE23 8FR, +44 (0)1332 640789, www.inderby.org.uk | Getting there A 30 minute-walk south from Derby bus station | Hours Daily Apr & May 8am–8pm, June–Aug 8am–9pm, Sept & Oct 8am–8pm, Nov–Mar 8am–6pm | Tip On the south side of the Arboretum, at 1 Wilfred Street, is Rose Hill House, a delightful neo-Elizabethan extravagance built in the 1830s complete with tall Tudor-style chimneys and decorative brickwork.

# 27 Derby Cathedral

*A flash of Georgian elegance*

Imposing medieval cathedrals dot the English landscape and attract most of the attention, leaving Derby Cathedral – more precisely the Cathedral Church of All Saints – under visited, which is a shame given that its subtle Georgian symmetries are a real delight. There has been a church here since the middle of the 10th century, but the original church tower was dismantled in 1510 to be replaced by the present structure a few years later. By any standard, this second tower is an impressive affair, comprising three stages adorned by a filigree of fine stone carving supported by slender buttresses and with battlements at the top.

By design, the soaring tower contrasts with the low-slung architecture of the adjacent church, which was itself built shortly after the original church was demolished in the 1720s. The architect was no less a figure than James Gibbs (1682–1754), a leading exponent of the Palladian style that was much favoured by Enlightenment figures such as Erasmus Darwin and Joseph Wright. Gibbs was also the man responsible for St Martin-in-the-Fields, a church of comparable design in London's Trafalgar Square. Gibbs conceived his Derby church as a parish church, but it was raised to cathedral status in 1927.

Inside the church, the broad sweep of the interior, with its pews, wooden gallery and fancy organ, is the epitome of Georgian elegance. Decoration is provided by an assortment of memorials, some of which are survivors from the original church, notably the tomb of Bess of Hardwick; others are *in situ*. In particular, look out for the memorial plaque dedicated to a certain Mary Chichester (d.1830), whose epitaph summarises some of the qualities expected of the ideal Georgian wife. There's also a memorial to the officers of the Derbyshire Regiment who died in a pair of shoddy imperial wars, the Crimean War and the Indian Mutiny.

**Address** 18–19 Iron Gate, Derby, DE1 3GP, +44 (0)1332 341201, www.derbycathedral.org | **Getting there** A 10-minute walk from Derby bus station | **Hours** Mon–Thu 8.30am–6.30pm, Fri 8.30am–5pm, Sat 9am–5pm, Sun 8.30am–6pm | **Tip** There are regular guided tours up the cathedral tower, but be warned there are nigh-on 200 steps. The views from the top over Derby are really rather grand. See website for further details.

# 28 Derby Council House

*Municipal polish*

Over the decades, many buildings in Derby have been bowdlerised or at least transformed by changes in taste and fashion – sometimes, as in the case of the Assembly Rooms on the Market Place, to the background of a loud groan from the locals. By comparison, the Council House, the large and really rather magisterial home of Derby City Council, has had things fairly easy, but it still stands as a beacon of former hopes and aspirations.

Few would argue that local government in the UK today seems penny-pinching and constrained, but in the 1930s, when work started on the Derby Central Improvement Scheme (CIP), there was a broader, more optimistic vision and this was reflected by both the style of the Council House and its location, in a prime and scenic spot on the banks of the River Derwent.

The man responsible for the design was the long-time borough architect Charles Herbert Aslin (1893–1959), a steadfast and reliable figure, the son of a Sheffield steelworker and a talented part-time artist to boot. In a future career, in Hertfordshire, Aslin would go on to pioneer the use of prefabricated school buildings, but here in Derby, the Council House was to be his set piece. It was built in the general style of the 18th century, its sombre symmetries of brown brick with stone dressings culminating in a large and architecturally assertive portico at the building's northwest corner. Looking as much like a Greek temple as a municipal headquarters, the portico's tall and slender columns are set beneath an extravagantly carved coat of arms plus a mini-balcony, as if the odd royal might be about to wave to the populace.

Aslin's design has survived almost in its entirety, although in 2011–22 some adjustments were made to the interior courtyard and a large glass screen was inserted into the western side of the building to improve lighting.

Address Corporation Street, Derby, DE1 2FS, www.derby.gov.uk | Getting there A 5-minute walk from Derby bus station | Hours Mon–Fri 9am–5pm | Tip The single-span, concrete Exeter Bridge next to the Council House was also partly designed by Aslin. It's decorated with pocket-sized bas-relief plaques celebrating Derby's great and good.

# 29 Derby Market Hall

*A Victorian covered market restored*

Reopened in the spring of 2025, Derby Market Hall is one of the city's finest buildings, an exercise in municipal self-confidence dating back to the 1860s. It was built at the insistence of the mayor, a certain Frederick Longdon, who felt that Derby's existing market facilities were way below par. His council colleagues fell into line and the hall was completed in three years at a cost of £29,000 (£2.4 million today). Longdon officiated at the opening ceremony during which a 600-strong choir performed Handel's *Messiah*.

Over the years, the Market Hall has been subject to various modifications, some sympathetic, others less so, but the recent refurbishment has kept to the spirit of the original building. Each of the Market Hall's several entrances is Italianate in style, the stone cladding intercepted by a balcony here and a tympanum or a fanlight window there. The approach from the Market Place is perhaps the most curious, along a columned passageway that burrows through the Guildhall. Inside, the Market Hall is simply splendid, with an arching, single-span roof of iron and glass balanced visually by a gallery that runs all the way round. The whole structure is supported on cast iron columns that were originally hollow to allow rain water to flush through them, an ingenious idea by the chief engineer, Rowland Mason Ordish (1824–1886), who went on to design the single-span roof of St Pancras station.

It is hoped that the revived Market Hall will bring together the best of the region's independent shopping, eating, drinking and entertainment. The food stalls already cover the gamut, from pancakes to pizza via jerk chicken, and there is ample space for events and activities. The hall re-opened just a few weeks before the writing of this book, so only time will tell how successful it will be, but it's a brave initiative – so let's hope it works.

**Address** Tennant Street, Derby, DE1 2DB, +44 (0)1332 255800, www.derbymarkethall.co.uk | **Getting there** Derby Market Hall is right in the city centre, footsteps from the Market Place and a 5-minute walk from the bus station | **Hours** Mon–Wed 8am–3pm, Thu–Sat 8am–10pm, Sun 11am–3pm | **Tip** Derby Market Hall is next door to the Guildhall and the Market Place, where you'll find the War Memorial and the *Derby Cascade*, a large and chunky art installation by William Pye (b. 1938). Pye is fond of his water sculptures, and although the locals have been hard to win over, they were irked when the water was switched off to save money in 2016.

# 30 Derby QUAD

*Sprucing up the Market Place*

Since the 1960s at least, planners, architects and politicians have been trying to improve Derby's sprawling Market Place. In the days of mass gatherings and giant, rough-and-tumble football games, the square was pretty much the perfect size – give or take the odd riot – but there was always a hankering for something more prestigious or at least cultural. Local cravings were ultimately soothed in the 1970s when the illustrious Hugh Maxwell Casson (1910–1999), the high priest of modern architecture, was brought to Derby to reimagine the square's centre piece, the Assembly Rooms.

Casson opted for a long and low-slung brutalist structure, whose radiator-like façade still stares blindly out across the square, though now it's from behind a fence: against the wishes of Casson's many fans and admirers, the Assembly Rooms await demolition. Things might have ended up differently if a fire had not damaged part of the complex in 2014; thereafter, the problems got worse and the money available for repairs and refurbishment got shorter.

This may all sound rather discouraging, but on the other side of the Market Square is the QUAD, a visually delightful and very popular structure perched partly on stilts and incorporating glass pods and stone cladding. Finished in 2008, the QUAD was designed by Feilden Clegg Bradley, an architectural partnership with a glowing reputation for sustainable designs and community awareness. The inside of the QUAD is busy, brisk and multi-purpose, beginning with a cinema that offers a lively programme of independent, off-beat and blockbuster films, all spiced up by film festivals like the full throttled horror of 'Darkness in the Fields'. QUAD also provides workshop space and puts on contemporary and modern art exhibitions with one recent offering being the excellent Dawn of Impressionism – in conjunction with the Musée d'Orsay.

Address Market Place, Derby, DE1 3AS, +44 (0)1332 290606, www.derbyquad.co.uk | Getting there A 5-minute walk from Derby bus station | Hours See the website for performance times | Tip Curiously, before Casson arrived, there was an 18th-century version of the Assembly Rooms. This was also damaged by fire and its façade was moved to Crich Tramway Village in the 1970s.

# 31 Derby Railway Roundhouse

*A magic roundabout*

Early steam locomotives were much happier travelling forwards than backwards – and indeed, the earliest couldn't travel backwards at all. This made railway turntables well-nigh essential and soon they were being installed within roundhouses, larger buildings where trains could be stored, serviced and repaired at the same time. Things moved doubly fast in train-town Derby where the greatest engineer of the day, Robert Stephenson (1803–1859), designed what was to be the first roundhouse in the world.

Stephenson was working for the North Midland Railway, as his father – George – had done before him, but it was a rackety, short-lived business and although Robert finished his commission, the company was soon to be subsumed within the Midland Railway.

Rackety or not, the result of Stephenson's endeavours, in 1839, was a splendid, 16-sided brick roundhouse with a cavernous timber-roofed interior that was big enough for multiple locomotives. It was lit from above, via a dome-shaped roof, which rose to a height of 50 feet, and it contained 16 lines of rails, radiating out from a turntable; the standard procedure was that an engine arrived, was shunted onto the turntable and then moved into any vacant stall from the 16 possible. A decade or so later, a sweet, vaguely Ruritanian clock tower was added to the roundhouse, but by then the Midland Railway had taken over the running of things.

Over the years, assorted railway works accumulated around the roundhouse, including a carriage shop, offices and an engine shop. Then, in a depressing sequence of events, British Rail Engineering Limited – as the works had become – was privatised in 1989 and closed in 1990. The buildings, including the roundhouse, soon deteriorated and only in 2000 was the site repurposed as part of the campus for Derby College.

**Address** The Roundhouse, 2 Roundhouse Road, Pride Park, Derby, DE24 8JE | **Getting there** Derby Railway Roundhouse is on the east side of Derby railway station; ask and you will be allowed to walk from one side of the station to the other via the footbridge spanning the train lines – this can be a useful short cut | **Hours** Core hours Mon–Fri 9am–5pm, but depends on events | **Tip** A new public body, Great British Railways, will soon run and plan the UK rail network. They will be based in Derby and have, as a first step, set up an office next to Derby train station – take a peek, though at present you can't pop in.

# 32 The Derby Ram

*A giant, ill-fated sheep*

In the middle of Derby, at the junction of East and Albion streets, is a chunky, somewhat lugubrious statue of a ram – or rather a semi-mythical version of a ram – by a modern British sculptor, Michael Pelger (b 1952). The sculpture, which was installed here in 1995, makes a gallant effort to conjure the gargantuan ram of Derbyshire folklore, hence its massive front legs, the extent of its heavy fleece and the sheer size of its curling horns. Some locals love it, others are more sceptical, but it is certainly true that the ram features prominently in Derby's history on several different levels. At its most straightforward, Derby County Football Club are called the Rams, and the local regiment of the British army has a ram as a mascot, but dig deeper and you soon enter the mists of ancient rites and rituals.

One particular thread is encapsulated by an old folk song entitled 'The Derby Ram' – or 'As I was Going to Derby'. Different versions have different lyrics, but they all feature an enormous ram with 'eagles nesting in its wool' and 'horns reaching up to the moon'. Neither does the song ever end well for the animal, who is butchered with some difficulty but without remorse: the shedding of its blood seems to be derived from Anglo-Saxon mid-winter fertility rites. The song even made it across the Atlantic – apparently George Washington could sing it.

A second thread is rather more convoluted, revolving round a local folk custom variously referred to as 'Old Tup', 'Derby Tup' or 'Derby Ram'. There were considerable variations as to what happened, but normally a band of villagers followed the central character, a man hidden by some sort of cape who 'rides' a hobby horse – a ram's head mounted on a pole. Some academics think that 'Old Tup' originated in the 17th century, others that the custom reaches back to the Greek god Pan, who was half man, half goat.

**Address** Junction of East Street and Albion Street, DE1 2AF | **Getting there** A 5-minute walk from Derby bus station | **Hours** Always accessible | **Tip** From the statue, it's an enjoyable 15-minute stroll over the River Derwent via the Exeter Bridge to the Smithfield, Riverlights House, Meadow Road, Derby, DE1 2BH (www.smithfieldderby.co.uk), a traditional riverside pub with a focus on beers from small breweries.

# 33 Derby the Railway Town

*Rolling stock Valhalla*

Drive along Derby's Litchurch Lane, near the city centre, and you'll pass several of the engineering plants that are still so important to Derby's economy. Among them, you'll spy the assorted brown-brick sheds and railway carriages of Alstom Transport, a French rolling stock manufacturer, which purchased the Litchurch works in 2021.

Alstom is but the latest owner of the works, which has changed hands with depressing regularity – and often to the detriment of the workforce – since the misguided privatisation of British Rail in the late 1980s and 1990s. Long gone are the days when Litchurch Lane was part of British Rail Engineering, whose multiple plants built and maintained British Rail's rolling stock. That said, the future is opaque: the British government seems committed to re-nationalising the railways and the new entity, 'Great British Railways', will be headquartered in Derby. Whether this will have any impact on the sourcing of the rolling stock remains to be seen.

The Litchurch works was separated out from other aspects of railway manufacture in the 1870s, becoming the place where rolling stock ('carriages and wagons') was built – not locomotives. There were breaks in both world wars, when the works switched to armaments, but otherwise its contribution to the industry has been enormous. It was here, for example, that they pioneered on-train sandboxes (the releasing of sand onto the track to improve traction) and it was here, in the 1950s, that they built the British Railways Mark 1 carriage, which was stronger and much safer than its predecessors.

Alstom is not in the habit of allowing public access to their Litchurch works, but in August, 2025, they opened the gates for a three-day 'Greatest Gathering' event to celebrate 200 years of railway history with lots of vintage stuff on display and rides on their test track. Watch out for repeats.

Address Alstom, Litchurch Lane, Derby, DE24 8AD, +44 (0)1332 344666, www.alstom.com | Getting there It's a somewhat circuitous 10-minute drive from Derby railway station to Alstom's Litchurch Lane works | Hours No regular hours – check website for visits and guided tours | Tip Great Northern Classics, on Osmaston Road, at the south end of Litchurch Lane, appeals to the car enthusiast with displays of – and events featuring – classic cars (www.greatnorthernclassics.co.uk).

# 34 Derby Theatre

*Professional theatre with university backing*

In the 1970s, Derby City Council together with the Arts Council worked with purpose to provide the city with a full-time professional theatre. The result was Derby Playhouse, a medium-sized (530-seater) theatre with a proscenium stage that was located in a new shopping centre, then the Eagle Centre, but now reincarnated as 'Derbion'. The first resident director was Mark Woolgar, who opened proceedings with *My Fair Lady* followed shortly afterwards by Chekhov's *The Seagull*, featuring Derby's own Alan Bates. In later years, the Derby Playhouse was to establish a glowing reputation for the quality of its musical theatre, but these salad days were not to last and the Playhouse was stricken with repeated financial crises in the early 2000s.

Matters came to a head in 2007 when, during the curtain call at the end of *Treasure Island*, it was announced that the Playhouse was going into liquidation. There was to be no return for the Playhouse, but the University of Derby picked up the threads, opening the 'Derby Theatre' in the same premises in 2009. As a stop-gap, the new theatre began with two Gilbert and Sullivan productions, but a new way forward was divined after the appointment of Sarah Brigham as artistic director in the early 2010s.

Today, Derby Theatre offers a varied and inventive programme headlined by leading modern playwrights – think Alan Ayckbourn and Amanda Whittington. This provides the superstructure for a highly regarded Learning Theatre programme, in which University of Derby students get the chance to work alongside professionals. Theatre students also get the chance to do their acting in front of live audiences – and there are plans to expand the number of studios available. Finally, the theatre works alongside a range of community groups with Derby Youth Musical Theatre's recent *Phantom of the Opera* being particularly successful.

Address Derby Theatre, 15 Theatre Walk, Derbion Shopping Centre, Derby, DE1 2NF, +44 (0)1332 593939 (box office), www.derbytheatre.co.uk | Getting there A 5-minute walk from Derby bus station | Hours For performance times and details, visit the website | Tip Derby Theatre is currently the only professional theatre in town, but this should change when the Guildhall (finally) re-opens. Derby has several amateur theatre companies, the best of which is probably the Derby Shakespeare Theatre Company (www.derbyshakespeare.org.uk).

# 35 Derby's Surrealist

*Marion Adnams at Derby Museum*

Often overlooked, Marion Elizabeth Adnams (1898–1995) was an inventive and talented painter, printmaker and draughtswoman, who was born in a trim Victorian terraced house at 22 Otter Street, on the northern edge of Derby. Her parents – her father was a woodwork teacher – taught her drawing and wood block printing and, at the same time, she prepared for her future by training as a language teacher. In the late 1920s, there was, however, a shift of emphasis after Adnams had spent time travelling in Belgium, France and Italy, making woodcuts of the architecture she encountered and then exhibiting them to rave reviews back home at Derby Art Gallery.

Marion hit her full artistic stride in the late 1930s after retraining as an art teacher. It was surrealism that inspired her, and although she never claimed to be part of the Surrealist movement, she came to her painting in a way that mirrored other Surrealists – via the close examination of natural objects, whose scale, colour and setting she could manipulate. The vigour of her *For Lo, Winter is Past* with its trio of gnarled trees is a case in point, as is the comparable *A Time to be Born and a Time to Die*. There are other bolder, arguably more vigorous, canvases too, with the sombre, fairy tale-like *L'Infante égarée* (*The Lost Infanta*) of 1944 a real stand-out – and clearly influenced by Magritte and Paul Delvaux.

From the 1930s onwards, Marion's surrealist work proved extremely popular and was widely and regularly exhibited across the UK, though failing eyesight obliged her to stop painting in 1968 just eight years after she had retired from teaching. Later, her estate bequeathed a raft of her paintings and sketches to the Derby Museum & Art Gallery, which displays a select part of this gift in a small but well-considered permanent exhibition entitled Marion Adnams: Into the Enchanted Country.

Address Derby Museum & Art Gallery, The Strand, Derby, DE1 1BS, www.derbymuseums.org | Getting there A 12-minute walk from Derby bus station | Hours Tue–Sat 10am–5pm, Sun noon–4pm | Tip The artist's childhood home at 22 Otter Street, Darley Abbey, Derby, DE1 3FB, is a 20-minute walk north of the bus station.

# 36 Derbyshire Cricket Ground

*To bowl or bat, that is the question*

The manicured lawns of Derbyshire County Cricket Ground lie a mile or so to the east of Derby Market Place, on the other side of the River Derwent. The ground has a long and eventful history, though its immediate surroundings are disappointingly drab and modern. More positively, the ground itself has an airy, almost village-like feel with few buildings crowding in on its boundary ropes, though a new four-storey media centre was opened in 2016.

Derbyshire County Cricket Club have been playing here since 1871 and although they have rarely hit the heights – they have only won the County Championship once, in 1936 – this is where visitors can feast on top-ranking cricket every season. The ground was also where a homeless Derby County Football Club played in the 1880s and 1890s and it was where England beat Ireland 9–0 in the British Home Championship of 1895 – a game well remembered in this author's family: my grandfather threw the hat of the man in front of him into the air to celebrate the first goal; he escaped retribution partly because of his protestations of innocence, but mainly on account of his clerical (dog) collar.

Derbyshire County Cricket Club has fielded many fine players over the years, including Dominic Cork, Mike Hendrick, Harold Rhodes and the wicketkeeper Bob Taylor. Derbyshire's speciality has always been bowlers, particularly fast bowlers, and bowlers tend to attract legends like magnets. One of the most beguiling is the story of the leg spinner Tommy Mitchell (1902–1996), a collier who supposedly learnt his skills practising with billiard balls. During the General Strike of 1926, Tommy was whiling away the hours bowling to his friends near Creswell Colliery where he worked, when a cricketer with contacts spotted him. Impressed by his action, the cricketer pushed his cause, and successful trials for Derbyshire and then England followed.

**Address** The County Ground, Nottingham Road, Chaddesden, Derby, DE21 6DA, +44 (0)1332 388101, www.cricket.derbyshireccc.com | **Getting there** A 20-minute walk from Derby bus station | **Hours** For cricket matches and events check the website | **Tip** Derbyshire are in Division 2 of the England and Wales Cricket County Championship. To see top-class, Division 1 cricket, the nearest ground is in Nottinghamshire (www.trentbridge.co.uk).

# 37 The Derwent Valley Line

*The charms of a branch line*

Amid the railway boom of the mid 19th century, Derbyshire was ripe for the plucking: there was coal to be moved from the pit heads, textiles from the mills, and limestone from the quarries of the Peak District. Neither was potential business limited to freight: Matlock Bath was wont to call itself 'Little Switzerland', with a stream of visitors who arrived by charabanc to see for themselves. Such lucrative prospects excited several railway companies, but their bitter rivalry was to delay the opening up of Derbyshire for years. Finally, in the 1860s, the rail line linking London with Derby, Matlock, Buxton and Manchester was opened and it soon became one of Midland Railway's prestige routes with the 10am 'Palatine Express' from Manchester Central to St Pancras a pre-war favourite.

Favourite or not, the line from Matlock to Buxton was closed in 1968, thanks to Dr Beeching's Axe. The rest of the line, running from Derby to Matlock, is today's Derwent Valley Line, whose assorted charms include a pair of vintage stations – Cromford is inordinately pretty – and trains that rattle through the centre (bowels) of Belper in dramatic style.

As far as the engineering was concerned, the first part of the route was easy enough, but the topography became more challenging as the railway approached Matlock. Fortunately, the chief engineer was the near-genius George Stephenson (1781–1848), who organised teams of miners to blast and tunnel their way through a prominent limestone cliff called High Tor. The miners worked from both ends and when they met they were, amazingly enough, just half an inch out of kilter.

Interestingly, the line from Matlock to Buxton presented a multitude of engineering problems as it pushed through the Peak District – but that didn't concern John Ruskin, who moaned that the railway meant 'every fool in Buxton can be in Bakewell in half an hour'.

Address The Derwent Valley Line begins at Derby railway station, Railway Terrace, Derby, DE1 2RU | Getting there Derby railway station is a 20-minute walk from Derby Market Place | Hours There are hourly trains from Derby to Matlock most of the time, with a journey time of about 30 minutes; for timetables, go to www.eastmidlandsrailway.co.uk | Tip A heritage railway, Peak Rail (www.peakrail.co.uk), extends the Derwent Valley Line north for 4 miles from Matlock to Rowsley.

# 38 Downtown by the Derwent

*Derby by the water*

In the centre of Derby, the agreeable Riverside Gardens string along the west bank of the River Derwent between the Holmes and Exeter bridges. The weir, the bend in the river, an overgrown islet, the assorted waterfowl and a set of folksy sculptures combine to make for an especially pleasant prospect – all supplemented by the distinctive, circular building that is the power-generating Longbridge Weir Hydro Power House.

A curving stone embankment frames and flanks the gardens as does Exeter Bridge, a sweeping, single span structure of reinforced concrete that was opened in 1931. The bronze medallions on the bridge celebrate local bigwigs like the silk man John Lombe and Erasmus Darwin, the grandfather of Charles.

A riverside path continues north from the Exeter Bridge, passing a marker for Exeter House, the mansion where Bonnie Prince Charlie bedded down during his brief stay here. Moving on, it's the shortest of strolls to the Cathedral Green Footbridge, whose modern design – with one leading mast – is certainly eye-catching if perhaps a little incongruous.

Within view of the footbridge and glued to the river bank is Derby's pride and joy, the Museum of Making. It's here that the River Derwent establishes its credentials as the cradle of the Industrial Revolution, its waters powering the mills that once hopscotched up the Derwent River Valley. Years ago, UNESCO designated the 15-mile stretch of river between Derby and Matlock Bath as the Derwent Valley Mills World Heritage Site and today this can be readily explored via the Derwent Valley Heritage Way. The latter is a popular, 55-mile waymarked footpath that begins at Derwent Mouth, at the confluence of the rivers Derwent and Trent, continues through the centre of Derby (via the railway station and Riverside Gardens) and ends up in the Peak District National Park.

Address Riverside Gardens, Derby, DE1 2BB | Getting there The Riverside Gardens begin a couple of minutes' walk from Derby bus station | Hours Always accessible | Tip From April to October, there are 45-minute boat cruises along the River Derwent on the Outram, a zero-emission, solar powered, electric boat. Departures are currently from Phoenix Green, near the Museum of Making. Bookings via www.derbycanal.org.uk/derby-river-boat-tickets.

# 39 Dracula at the Grand

*Vampires ahoy*

Babington Lane, in the centre of Derby, is really rather humdrum, but, if you keep your eyes peeled, you can spot the attractive, Italian Renaissance-style façade of the old Grand Theatre at number nine: the name survives in lettering on the upper level, even though the ground floor has been bowdlerised as the 'House of Holes' – adults-only crazy golf would you believe? Opened in 1886 with a capacity of 2,500, the Grand has had a varied history, firstly as a theatre, then as the Locarno ballroom – all beehive hair-dos and Elnett hair spray – and more recently as a Chinese restaurant.

The Grand's particular – perhaps peculiar – claim to fame dates to 1924, when it witnessed the very first performance of *Dracula*, which was itself the first authorised adaptation of Bram Stoker's eponymous 1897 novel. The play was written by Hamilton Deane (1880–1958), an Irish playwright and actor who capitalised on old family connections to persuade Stoker's widow and energetic literary executor, Florence Balcombe (1858–1937), to grant him dramatic rights.

In a stroke of genius, Deane transformed Count Dracula into an urbane sophisticate, a socialite dressed in a formal dinner suit beneath a flowing, high-collared opera cape. It was the cape that came to epitomise Dracula more than anything else, though initially it was conceived mainly as a stage prop, concealing the actor while he slipped through a trap-door in the stage floor. The play was a huge success and toured for years – with and without the added bonus of a uniformed nurse on hand to administer smelling salts should anyone be overwhelmed. The play crossed the Atlantic in 1927 and it was here that the Hungarian actor Bela Lugosi played the Count – as he did in the classic Tod Browning *Dracula* film of 1931, but still without the fangs: these only arrived with the 1958 Hammer Films version starring Christopher Lee.

**Address** 9 Babington Lane, Derby, DE1 1TA | **Getting there** A 10-minute walk from Derby bus station | **Hours** Exterior always visible | **Tip** From the Grand Theatre, it's a 5-minute walk to the Green Lane conservation area and its assortment of imposing Victorian buildings. The star turn here was the Derby Hippodrome, at 80 Green Lane and Macklin Street, but this grand, derelict structure had to be demolished in 2025.

# 40 Duffield Castle

*Disappearing castles*

Hugging the A6 about six miles north of Derby, pocket-sized Duffield has been inhabited since at least the Iron Age and it was here that Roman baggage trains crossed the River Derwent carrying lead from Wirksworth bound for Deventio (Roman Derby) and points beyond. William the Conqueror ceded land here to one of his most powerful Norman followers, Henry de Ferrers, and the family soon plonked timber fortifications on a prominent sandstone ridge overlooking the river valley.

In the musical chairs of medieval England, the fortunes of the owners of Duffield Castle varied widely: William I de Ferrers (died 1190), was punished for joining a rebellion against Henry II, whereas his son, William II de Ferrers (1168–c.1247), benefitted from being one of King John's favourites. It was during this period that Duffield Castle was rebuilt in stone, the original motte and bailey replaced by a massive keep. Yet things soon went wrong. Plagued by gout, the irascible Robert de Ferrers (1239–1279), was both violent and politically maladroit, a lethal combination in the swirling uncertainties of the reign of Henry III (1207–1272). Robert joined in one unsuccessful rebellion and was pardoned, but failed to take the hint and rebelled again. This time he was imprisoned and Duffield Castle was demolished with much of the stone being scavenged by locals.

The Castle may have disappeared, but vague memories of its existence persisted with the site being given to the National Trust in 1899. Since then, there have been several archaeological digs with the main surprise being just how large the stone keep was – roughly 98 by 95 feet. Today, there's nothing much to see, except the scant remains of some foundations and the dome-shaped stone cover that tops off an ancient well, but the site has a pleasant, glade-like feel and you can let your imagination do the rest.

Address Duffield Castle, Milford Road, Duffield, DE56 4DW, +44 (0)1332 842191, www.nationaltrust.org.uk | Getting there A flight of steps leads up from Milford Road (A6) to Duffield Castle – watch for the National Trust sign, about 6 miles north of Derby (no parking on the main road, so you'll have to opt for one of the nearby side streets); train to Duffield railway station, then a 10-minute walk; bus 6X from Derby and Belper | Hours Dawn–dusk during summer months; check website for winter opening | Tip Duffield railway station is pretty and cute – its platform gardens immaculate in spring and summer.

# 41 Electric Daisy

*Derby at its most inventive*

Bright, cheerful and very welcoming, the Electric Daisy bills itself as a 'seed for city-wide rejuvenation' and as 'proof that with shared purpose, we can turn forgotten spaces into flourishing hubs of community and culture'. Who could possibly argue with those morale-raising ambitions? And indeed the Electric Daisy has put to excellent use a neglected corner of the city centre, a space that had become a dispiritingly tatty car park, a stone's throw from Derby Museum & Art Gallery. To begin with, the Electric Daisy site was levelled, then a good lick of (pink) paint was administered, plants and shrubs in tubs were introduced, and finally there were the furnishings – benches, tables, parasols and so forth; future plans have proposed the use of a pink stainless-steel shipping container as a bar and a Cruck tent for outdoor events, the Cruck tent being a freestanding, timber structure with a transparent roof.

Opened in June 2023, the Electric Daisy is the flagship enterprise of 'Down To Earth Derby', whose founder is local lad Jamie Quince-Starkey, a one-time Rolls-Royce employee with a keen interest in both the environment and the creative arts. It is perhaps this combination of interests that gives the Electric Daisy its variety and it does seem to cater for pretty much everyone and everything, from live music, and pop-up markets, through to outdoor movie nights, theatre workshops, DJ nights, family-friendly days, kids' parties, birthday parties and garden brunches.

Prudently, Quince-Starkey has taken advice from Cornwall's Eden Project and he seems well on the way to creating a space where 'art, greenery and bold ideas thrive'. To this author at least, it seems a little unlikely that this creative bonhomie will spread through the wider community, but it would be churlish not to wish him the best of luck.

Address 1–4 Bold Lane, Derby, DE1 3NT, www.electricdaisy.org | Getting there A 12-minute walk from Derby bus station | Hours Community garden Fri 4–8pm, Sat noon–8pm; check website for details of events, open days and workshops | Tip Across the street from the Electric Daisy is St Werburgh's Church, an ungainly edifice that mostly dates from the early 18th century. This was where Samuel Johnson (1709–1784) took a little time out from his dictionary making to get married in 1735.

# 42 Elvaston Castle and Park

*Nude wrestling with Alan and Oliver*

In March 1830, William Barron (1805–1891) was appointed head gardener at Elvaston Castle by Charles Stanhope, the 4th Earl of Harrington (1780–1851), who had just moved in. Now this particular earl, commonly known as 'Beau' Petersham, was an influential figure, a dandy among dandies, whose affectations were observed and even mimicked by the Prince Regent and his hangers-on: Petersham spoke with a kind of lisp, so others followed; he had 365 snuff boxes, there was a rush on snuff boxes; and he fixated on tea and everyone else did too.

If Barron had any misgivings as to his new employer, they are not recorded, but in the event the partnership between the two was a great success: the earl wanted to see his gardens blossom as speedily as possible and it turned out that Barron was a wizard at transplanting mature trees. Slowly, news of Barron's genius spread far and wide with his status as a horticultural hero assured by the 1852 publication of his *British Winter Garden*, which promoted the use of evergreens in public and private spaces.

Though much has changed since Barron worked here, strolling through the gardens at Elvaston remains a delight. There are formal gardens and topiary galore on one side of the house, woods, an artificial lake, 'romantic' rock follies and mini grottoes on another. By comparison, the house – the 'castle' – is something of a mixed bag. Low slung and castellated, it looks rather confused, which indeed it is, the Elizabethan original redesigned and extended in Gothic Revival style in the 19th century. Inside, the highlight is the Gothic Hall, the 'Hall of Fair Star' (meaning his wife, Maria) as the fourth earl called it in a daft attempt to prove how romantic he was. It was here in this room, with a log fire blazing, that Ken Russell shot the nude wrestling scene between Oliver Reed and Alan Bates in the 1969 film *Women in Love*.

**Address** Elvaston Castle and Country Park, Borrowash Road, Elvaston, Derby, DE72 3EP, +44 (0)1629 533870, www.derbyshire.gov.uk | **Getting there** 8 miles from Derby via the B5010 – there's parking inside the park near the castle, which is yards from St Bartholomew's Church | **Hours** The Castle is only open to the public on guided tours; to book, go to www.elvastonestate.org.uk; gardens are open daily 1 Nov–31 Mar 9am–5pm, 1 Apr–31 Oct 9am–8pm | **Tip** Elvaston is just 5 miles from Chellaston, now a suburb of Derby, but once famous across Europe for its quarries, which produced the easy-to-carve alabaster that was used in thousands of religious sculptures.

# 43 Eyam and the Plague

*The Mompessons: bravery in adversity*

Within a year of September, 1665, the solitary lead-mining settlement of Eyam, 35 miles north of Derby, had lost half of its population of 750 to the bubonic plague, a calamity that earned it the enduring epithet 'The Plague Village'. The first victim was one George Viccars, a journeyman tailor who is said to have released some infected fleas into his lodgings from a bale of cloth he had brought here from London.

Acutely conscious of the danger to neighbouring villages, William Mompesson, the village rector, speedily organised a self-imposed quarantine, arranging for food to be left at places on the parish boundary. Payment was made with coins left in pools of disinfecting vinegar in holes chiselled into the old boundary stones. The rector even closed the church and held services in the open air at a natural rock arch to the south of the village – Cucklet Delph. Mompesson himself survived the plague, though his wife did not; he remarried four years later.

Nowadays, Eyam is a good-looking village whose main street is flanked by old stone houses. It takes a few hours to explore the place properly, beginning with the church of St Lawrence, on the main street, where informative panels delve into the village's plague history; outside, in the graveyard, stands the distinctive table tomb of Mompesson's wife, Catherine, whose tireless work nursing sick villagers was long remembered. Further along the street are the 'plague cottages' where a series of garden plaques reveal who died where, though the most harrowing memorial is perhaps the Riley Graves, in open country just east of the village along Riley Lane. They commemorate Elizabeth Hancock, who buried her husband, three sons and three daughters within the space of eight days.

North of the village is Eyam Museum, with more on the plague and Mompesson's Well, where money was once swapped for provisions.

Address St Lawrence's Church, Church Street, Eyam, Hope Valley, S32 5QH, www.achurchnearyou.com/church/13176 | Getting there Eyam is 35 miles from Derby on the A619; train to Grindleford then a half-hour walk or short bus ride | Hours St Lawrence's Church Mon–Sat 10am–4pm, Sun 12.30–4pm; Riley Graves and Mompesson's Well are always accessible | Tip Eyam Hall, Main Road, Eyam (www.eyamhall.co.uk), is a manor house dating from the 17th century. It's often open to the public as are its gardens. They have a café here too.

# 44 Foremark Nature Reserve

*Country rambles*

Built in the 1970s, Foremark Reservoir, about 14 miles south of Derby, is shaped something like a heart, its deepish waters mostly constrained by concrete walls and a dam. The reservoir is sourced from the River Dove and its main purpose is to guarantee the water supply for Leicester. Severn Trent owns the reservoir and its immediate surroundings, but things are currently in a state of transition as the National Trust have been managing the property since 2022. Severn Trent is deeply unpopular with many locals, so this joint venture has not been universally welcomed, but to be fair the National Trust has used the opportunity to improve Foremark's facilities. There are picnic tables, a café and an adventure playground – though visitors are not allowed to dip their toes never mind swim in the reservoir waters.

The Nature Reserve surrounding the reservoir is large enough for several different sorts of habitat, principally woodland and grass heathland. Two short and easy walks have been laid out on the east side of the water – the Green Walk (1.5 miles) and the Orange Walk (3.5 miles). Foremark is also within the National Forest, that heartening attempt to plant thousands of trees across some of the most damaged and ravaged post-industrial landscapes of the Midlands. Stage 5 (4 hours; 7.5 miles) of the 75-mile long National Forest Way (www.nationalforest.org) runs through Foremark *en route* from Ashby-de-la-Zouch to Ticknall.

Other options include a good old hoof down to the marshy Carvers Rocks at the very southern tip of the reservoir or the 3.5 mile drive to Heath Wood on Ingleby Lane followed by a woodland walk. There are no signs in Heath Wood to indicate where they are, but archaeologists have unearthed 59 Viking burial barrows here, the remains of invaders from the Great Heathen Army that reached Repton in A.D. 873.

Address Foremark Nature Reserve (NT), Milton, DE65 6EG, +44 (0)1332 863822, www.nationaltrust.org.uk | Getting there Foremark is a 14-mile drive southwest of Derby and is accessible from the road between Milton and Ticknall (A514) | Hours Opening hours vary with the seasons – check the National Trust website | Tip There is no village of Foremark as such, but there is Foremark Hall, a grandiose 18th-century pile about four miles north of the reservoir and now occupied by Repton School.

# 45 Foulds Guitars

*Guitar specialist and live music mainstay*

Good quality, specialist shops are always a treat when you discover them and Foulds Guitars, in attractive premises in Derby's Strand Arcade, is no exception. It was way back in 1893 that the original Charles Foulds opened his first store in Nottingham. He decamped to Derby a few years later, setting up shop on Iron Gate, where the Foulds and their shop stayed until James Foulds retired in 2018.

Now under new management in new premises, Foulds spreads its musical expertise deep and wide, its reassuringly knowledgeable staff guiding customers who have every degree of aptitude and experience imaginable – from full-time professional musicians through to occasional strummers and everything in between.

The Foulds shop possesses three showrooms and, taken together, they hold a first-rate selection of guitars, both new and used. Part-exchange is possible and they also have a full repair and reconditioning service. Many customers are keen to check out their vintage guitars, and recent offerings have included a Fender 72 Thinline Telecaster Natural for £900, a 1966 Telecaster for £14,000, and a Rickenbacker 4003/5 for £2,500. Foulds also does great side lines in a variety of other musical instruments – also both new and used – including ukuleles, banjos, harmonicas, mandolins and keyboards. And then there's all the associated recording equipment, amps and related paraphernalia.

Over the years, the contribution Foulds has made to the Derby music scene is inestimable. They bolster this by having an in-house teaching room and by listing local music teachers on their website: Ethan Fitzgerald, for example, works in the shop and teaches guitar, specialising in Rock music, while Mary Prince does drums – Funk and Rock. As for famous Derby guitarists, you might kick off with Anthony Franklin (Whitesnake) and Duncan Lloyd (Maximo Park).

**Address** 3–4 The Strand Arcade, The Strand, Derby, DE1 1BQ, +44 (0)1332 342456, www.fouldsguitars.com | **Getting there** A 10-minute walk from Derby bus station | **Hours** Mon–Sat 10am–5.30pm | **Tip** If you can't find what you want at Foulds, you might wend your way over to Rattle & Drum Music, 79 Osmaston Road (www.rattleanddrum.com), or the adjacent second-hand musical instrument shop, Hippo Guitars, at 81 Osmaston Road (www.hippoguitars.com). Both are a 10-minute walk away.

# 46 Friar Gate Bridge

*A handsome Victorian railway bridge*

In the 1870s, during a railway boom, the Great Northern Railway (GNR) decided to expand its network by building the Derbyshire and Staffordshire Extension – in the teeth of opposition by the rival Midland Railway. The new line was an ambitious undertaking that involved the digging of several tunnels, the construction of two viaducts – including the Bennerley Viaduct – and the demolition of houses in Derby on and around Friar Gate, where there was to be a station, a goods yard and a bridge.

Reassuringly, the GNR was accustomed to such large projects and in Richard Johnson (1827–1924) they had a chief engineer who knew exactly what he was doing. Nonetheless, the well-heeled folk of Friar Gate disliked the whole idea of a railway passing through their back yard and so, trying to appease them, Johnson asked a local iron foundry, Andrew Handyside & Co., to design a stylish Friar Gate bridge. The result was an elegant, single span, cast-iron structure comprising two nearly parallel, double-track bridges that separated as they approached the new railway station. The bridge had impressive-looking dressed stone abutments and intricately moulded parapets and spandrels that contained a deer motif like the one on the city's coat of arms. If Johnson thought he had placated his local foes, however, he was mistaken, with one railing about the 'meretricious decoration, which only emphasised the insult'. No free tickets for him then.

The Friar Gate line closed in the 1960s, since when the station and associated track have all but disappeared, but not the bridge, which has been effectively topped and tailed, leaving the bridge and its abutments a somewhat isolated memorial to the great age of the railways. At time of writing, this part of Friar Gate is being redeveloped with both the bridge and the nearby – and now derelict – Goods Yard scheduled to benefit.

Address 36 Friar Gate, Derby, DE1 1DA | Getting there A 15-minute walk from Derby bus station | Hours Always accessible | Tip In World War II, no singers were more popular than Flanagan and Allen, whose best-known song – 'Underneath the Arches' – was written in Derby after Flanagan observed the homeless sleeping under Friar Gate Bridge.

# 47 Friar Gate Delights

*Georgian architecture and a splash of modern art*

A long sequence of handsome Georgian houses stretches out along the north side of Friar Gate, extending from the Friar Gate Bridge and the neighbouring Pickford's House as far as Vernon Street. Particular high points on the way include the intricate brickwork of number 45 and the softly hued, reddish brickwork and delicate neo-classical doorway of the house next door. There's yet more of interest on the other side of the street, at the foot of the plane tree in front of 83 Friar Gate. It's here you'll spot a tight cluster of partially buried and skilfully sculpted ceramic heads, an appealing modern sculpture by the artist Tim Clapcott.

The sculpture is called the *Reform Bill Heads* and it commemorates the Derby rioters who took to the streets in 1831. Parliament had refused to extend voting rights and, when news of this spread, hundreds gathered in Derby Market Place to object. Angry, the crowd attacked the houses of well-known opponents of reform and then moved on to the Friar Gate prison, where they forced entry by using one of Derby's new cast-iron lampposts as a battering ram – not at all what the city fathers had in mind when they proudly installed them. A number of prisoners were liberated, including several previously incarcerated rioters – hence the location of the Clapcott sculpture just across Friar Gate.

The prison that stood at Friar Gate 47–51 was demolished in the early 19th century and the good-looking replacement dwellings you see today date to the 1840s. Yet the builders left much of the basement pretty much untouched and a set of prison cells (at nos. 50 and 51) has survived, some of them with the original doors and graffiti. These cells are now a privately run tourist attraction with entry down a flight of steps at the front of the current building.

It is claimed that the prison is haunted.

Address Outside 83 Friar Gate, Derby, DE1 1DA | Getting there A 15-minute walk from Derby bus station | Hours Friar Gate is always accessible | Tip Derby Ghost Walk and Jail, 50–51 Friar Gate, is operated as a tourist attraction by Richard Felix (www.richardfelix.co.uk).

# 48 The Guildhall

*Victorian solemnity*

Standing tall and proud on Derby's Market Place, the 1840s Guildhall is the second edition – the first version had been badly damaged by fire. The architects were Duesbury & Lee, who added a large domed clock tower to the original and expanded the building's façade, the end result being a sort of heavy-duty mix of classical Greek and Italian Renaissance styles. The sobriety of the whole ensemble was greatly admired by Derby's Victorian bourgeoisie and the Guildhall soon became a local landmark – and even today it has a certain ponderous charm. The replacement façade also carried two relief panels with the one on the left representing judicial proceedings, the other municipal proceedings. Both are well executed and dynamic, the work of one of the era's most popular public sculptors, John Bell (1811–1895).

The original 1820s building had been the work of Matthew Habershon (1789–1852), a curiously earnest chap whose evangelical Christianity brought him to the notice of the equally devout king of Prussia, Friedrich Wilhelm IV (1795–1861). The king dipped into the royal cupboard to award Habershon all sorts of trinkets and baubles, even giving him a gold medal for his page-turner *The Ancient Half-timbered Houses of England*.

Until 1954, the Guildhall's Council Chamber was the site of council meetings, but in the early 1970s this was turned into the cosy and intimate Guildhall Theatre. Sadly, the theatre has been closed since 2019, and although there now seems to be money enough to open things up again, seeing is believing. More positively, the adjacent Market Hall has now been re-opened after a major refit and can be reached – among several entrances – via a vaulted passageway running through the Guildhall. In the meantime, until the theatre re-opens, you can expect the Guildhall to turn ever greener with the growth of assorted mosses and lichens.

**Address** Market Place, Derby, DE1 3AS | **Getting there** A 5-minute walk from Derby bus station | **Hours** Exterior always visible | **Tip** The unusually flamboyant, half-timbered house two doors down from the Guildhall marks the spot where an early pioneer of gynaecology, Dr Percival Willoughby (1596–1685), had his surgery.

# 49 Handyside Bridge

*Functional elegance*

Born in Edinburgh, Andrew Handyside (1805–1887) was one of those restless, energetic entrepreneurs who powered so much of the Victorian age for both good and evil. In 1848, recognising that Derby was a burgeoning rail town, Handyside bought a local iron foundry, gauging that there were more profits to be made from both the existing product range, comprising the likes of stoves and baths, window frames, vases and urns, and from new, larger stuff – bridges in particular. Handyside took to selling his wares across Britain and the Empire and nor did he rest on his technological haunches, diversifying his foundry by adding first a brass foundry and then a malleable cast iron foundry where cast iron could be made much less brittle by means of a heat treatment.

In the 1870s, after a struggle with the Midland Railway, a new Great Northern Railway (GNR) line from Nottingham was approaching Derby, but first it had to span the River Derwent. The GNR turned to Richard Johnson (1827–1924), their talented and reliable chief engineer, for a plan and as ever he came up trumps. Johnson plumped for a riveted, wrought-iron bridge with a single-span of 140 feet, 16 feet high at the centre, and supported by a pair of bow-shaped trusses. Crucially, the design meant that there was no need for a supporting pier in the water and thus no impediment to navigation on the River Derwent. Today, the wrought-iron makes the bridge look solid and almost indestructible, but it's only from the side – with the river below – that you can really appreciate its elegant charm.

Handyside completed the bridge, on what was commonly called the Friargate Line, in 1878. In the late 1960s, the line was axed and the track was ripped up with the bridge, now a footbridge, becoming an entrance to that sweep of parkland that stretches north along the River Derwent as far as Darley Abbey Mills.

**Address** Darley Abbey, Derby, DE1 3FB | **Getting there** From Derby Market Place, it's a 20-minute walk to Handyside Bridge | **Hours** Always accessible | **Tip** Handyside Bridge forms part of the Derwent Valley Mills World Heritage Site. The next bridge downstream is St Mary's Bridge, which is 500 metres away, and the next bridge upstream is the pedestrian-only Darley Abbey bridge, which is about 1,5 kilometres away.

# 50 The Hanson Log Boat

*Bronze Age cruising*

Some 66 miles long, the River Derwent slices through the centre of Derby before worming its way southeast to join the River Trent, that great waterway of the East Midlands. Traders and invaders have been using this river system for centuries, but it was still something of a surprise when a huge, 32-foot prehistoric log boat was discovered near Derby in 1998. Dating from the Middle Bronze Age, about 1500 B.C., the log boat was made from a single, hollowed-out oak tree trunk. Close examination indicated that flint and antler tools had been used to shape both the outside and the inside of the boat, while heated stones were used in the hollowing out too. There was also some evidence of birch strips being used for ongoing repairs, each strip held in place with oak wedges, and even the remains of the boat's last cargo, locally quarried sandstone, thought to have been bound for the strengthening of a causeway across the River Trent.

The log boat was unearthed during quarrying at a gravel pit in Shardlow, some nine miles southeast of Derby. 'Hanson' was the name of the company who owned the gravel pit, hence the name. After its discovery, the boat's conservation proved far from easy. Sunk beneath the gravel, its waterlogged condition had preserved the wood, but made it extremely fragile – so, after much huffing and puffing, the boat was sawn into pieces and transported to York, where it was immersed in polyethylene glycol for over a year to strengthen the timber; only then could the log boat be dried out and made safe for display.

Today, the log boat is one of the prize exhibits at Derby Museum and Art Gallery – and it's a rare find too: only a handful of Bronze Age boats have ever been discovered in the UK and the majority are made of oak planks sewn together rather than hollowed-out tree trunks. Which was the more effective design, it's hard to say.

Address Derby Museum and Art Gallery, The Strand, Derby, DE1 1BS, +44 (0)1332 641901, www.derbymuseums.org | Getting there A 12-minute walk from Derby bus station | Hours Tue–Sat 10am–5pm, Sun noon–4pm | Tip A second and very similar log boat was discovered near the first in 2003. The boat was investigated and reburied, whereas the two Clifton Log Boats, discovered in neighbouring Nottinghamshire, were retrieved and are displayed by Nottingham Museums (www.nottinghasmmuseums.org.uk).

# 51 Hardwick Hall

*A magnificent Elizabethan mansion*

Hardwick Hall is a stunningly beautiful country house some 23 miles north of Derby. It owes its existence to Elizabeth Hardwick (1527–1608), aka Bess of Hardwick, who rose to become one of the leading lights of Elizabethan England despite being born the daughter of a minor Derbyshire squire. Bess had a love of building, and Hardwick Hall, begun when she was 62, has survived in exquisite condition. At the time, the house was the epitome of fashionable taste, a balance of symmetry and ingenious detail, in which the crisp lines of the building are offset by a multiplicity of windows – there's actually more glass than stone – while up above, the countess' giant-sized initials (E. S.) intercept every roof line.

Inside, a special highlight is the top-floor High Great Chamber, where Bess received her most distinguished guests. It was here that she installed a fine plaster frieze that celebrated the goddess Diana, the virgin huntress – with the intention of pleasing the Virgin Queen herself. Next door, the Long Gallery is similarly gorgeous, from the splendid chimneypieces and tapestries through to a set of portraits, including one each of the queen and Bess. Bess and her friends could exercise here while keeping out of the sun – any hint of a tan was then considered distinctly plebeian.

Look out also for the hall's large collection of antique needlework, including several pieces by Mary, Queen of Scots, who was held in custody for 15 years by the last of Bess' four husbands, the Earl of Shrewsbury. He moaned about the expense incessantly – one reason for the souring of his relationship with Bess and their subsequent estrangement. Outside, the garden makes for a pleasant wander and, beyond the ha-ha (the animal-excluding ditch and low wall), rare breeds of cattle and sheep graze the surrounding parkland. Bess was buried in All Saints Church, now Derby Cathedral.

**Address** Doe Lea, Chesterfield, S44 5QJ, but for Satnavs use S44 5RW, +44 (0)1246 850430, www.nationaltrust.org.uk | **Getting there** 23 miles north of Derby via the A38 and then the M1 – follow the signs from exit 29; train to Chesterfield then taxi for the last 9 miles | **Hours** Check the website for seasonal opening hours | **Tip** It is perhaps a little confusing, but before Bess built Hardwick Hall, she lived in the adjacent Hardwick Old Hall, now a substantial if broken-down ruin operated by English Heritage (www.english-heritage.org.uk).

# 52 Hathersage: David Mellor

*The finest cutlery in the land*

Born in Sheffield, David Mellor (1930–2009) was a brilliant designer, one of the finest of his generation. He began by designing and making silverware before opening a shop in London's Sloane Square that sold a range of kitchenware and tableware. Yet his self-imposed mission was much wider than that: he had a strong and quintessentially democratic desire to improve design standards over society as a whole, making life for the majority both easier and more comfortable. And his commissions were remarkably varied, including the designing of a safer traffic light system and better bus stops, though his first love was always metalwork and associated skills.

Mellor began manufacturing cutlery in the 1970s, but he stepped up a gear when he decided to open his own cutlery factory in Hathersage, an hour's drive from Derby. Mellor's serious intent was echoed by his choice of architect, Michael Hopkins (1935–2023), a major figure in his own right and well known for designs that blended tradition with modernity. Hopkins built the new factory on the circular foundations of Hathersage's defunct gas works – and the Round Building opened in 1990. It's a beautiful building too, made of stone with a conical lead roof and central lantern, and it's now surrounded by mature trees.

David Mellor's son, Corin, has taken over the company and is responsible for its evolution at Hathersage. Behind the Round Building now is a miniature street scene illustrating Mellor's various design contributions plus a collection of buildings including a free museum and a café serving a wide range of delicious food. Here also is a deluxe shop selling kitchen knives and boards, tableware, glassware, craft pottery, woodware and kitchen essentials, but the showstopper is the Mellor cutlery, stainless steel, silver plate and sterling silver, and always breathtakingly beautiful.

Address The Round Building, Leadmill, Hathersage, Hope Valley, S32 1BA, +44 (0)1433 650220, www.davidmellordesign.com | Getting there Hathersage is about 38 miles from Derby via the A38 | Hours Mon–Sat 10am–5pm, Sun 11am–5pm (factory tours on Sundays – reservations recommended but not essential; tours last 30–45 minutes) | Tip Hathersage is within easy striking distance of some wonderfully wild scenery – you might start with the National Trust's Padley Gorge.

# 53 Heage Windmill

*Explore a Georgian windmill*

The scattered village of Heage, about 12 miles north of Derby, spreads over the hills above the industrial – and post-industrial – towns that string along the Derbyshire/Nottinghamshire border. The village's name comes from the Old English for 'high ridge' and it certainly has an airy, open location – a little too open for its inhabitants in 1645 when a freakish storm all but destroyed the village church; the storm came in the middle of the Civil War, so both sides blamed the other for the loss of God's favour.

The main reason to visit today is Heage Windmill, a handsome structure glued to a hillside on the northern edge of the village. Built in the 1790s, this is a 'tower mill', comprising a sturdy stone tower on top of which is a cap for rotating the sails. The tower was built on an ironstone outcrop, which was partly quarried for its construction. The windmill started with just four sails, but Thomas and Isaac Shore, the brothers who bought it in the 1850s, added a 'fantail', a mini windmill mounted behind and at right angles to the sails; this turned the cap to bring it into the wind.

Storms are a constant danger to all windmills and Heage's cap and sails were blown off in 1894. Yet the Shores were undeterred, doing the repairs and increasing the number of sails to six – as they remain today. In 1919, Heage Windmill lost its fantail in yet another storm and this time, the owner, another Shore, gave up and closed the windmill down. Years of neglect followed, but in 1968 Derbyshire County Council rode to the rescue and restoration work began. A charitable trust now supervises the windmill, which has been fully operational since 2002. Visitors are offered an enjoyable guided tour and can buy some of the flour made here in the shop. There is also a programme of special events with vehicles often prominent – a 'Land Rovers Drop In', for example.

**Address** Chesterfield Road, Heage, Belper, DE56 2BH, +44 (0)1773 853579, www.heagewindmill.org.uk | **Getting there** Heage Windmill is about 12 miles from Derby off the B6013 | **Hours** Apr–Oct Sat & Sun plus Bank Holidays 11am–4pm; guided tours available | **Tip** From the windmill, it's 3 miles to Butterley, where the old railway station is at the beginning of a long process that should turn it into a heritage railway (www.midlandrailway-butterley.co.uk).

# 54_Iron Gate

*Victorian salad days*

Arguably Derby's best-looking thoroughfare, Iron Gate runs south to north through the city centre beginning at the Market Place and ending beside the cathedral. In Victorian times, Iron Gate was busy and fashionable in equal measure and, although much of the gloss has worn off, the street is still flanked by a platoon of handsome, old buildings. Proceeding north along Iron Gate, one of the first structures of any real charm is the ornate, 18th-century brick building at the junction with Sadler Gate; here, a pretty little porch supported by twin stone columns once served as a suitably inviting entrance to a Lloyds Bank.

Just along the street, Wetherspoons have arrived in the form of the Standing Order pub, at number 28. All credit to the pub chain for their tasteful recycling of a grand old bank, designed in a forceful Italianate style – of brick with stone facings – in the 1870s. The architect was Birmingham's Julius Alfred Chatwin (1830–1907), the great-grandfather of that most elusive of travel writers, Bruce Chatwin (1940–1989). On the other (east) side of the street, at number 11, the Slug and Lettuce occupies an imposing building whose expansive stone façade dates from the 1870s; designed as top-ranking offices, the building comes complete with four banks of windows and fancy double gates.

A few yards away, the stone arch adjacent to Pizza Express sports a blue plaque dedicated to John Whitehurst (1713–1788), the inventor, who lived and worked here for almost 30 years. The son of a Cheshire clockmaker, Whitehurst moved to Derby, where he established his own business designing all manner of scientific instruments from thermometers and barometers through to hydraulics. Every inch a figure of the Enlightenment, Whitehurst was an important member of the Birmingham Lunar Society, whose influential tentacles spread right across Derbyshire.

**Address** Iron Gate, Derby, DE1 3GP | **Getting there** A 10-minute walk from Derby bus station | **Hours** Always accessible | **Tip** While you're exploring Iron Gate, keep an eye out for the modest and modern Orrery Memorial sculpture celebrating Joseph Wright's orrery painting; it's outside no. 34.

# 55 Joan Wast Memorial

*A Protestant martyr at the Windmill Pit*

The 1550s were cruel and bitter times in England. In 1553, Queen Mary (1516–1558) came to the throne determined to stop the Protestant Reformation in its tracks and return the country to the Pope. The following year, she had the Heresy Acts revived and, in fear for their lives, many Protestants fled abroad, though this was not an option for poor 'heretics' like Derby's Joan Wast (or Waste).

Born blind in 1534, Joan learnt to knit and make ropes – her father was a ropemaker – but it was then that religion transformed her life: during the reign of Edward VI (1537–1553), the Bible was read in English in churches for the first time – only Latin had been permitted before. Joan was inspired by what she heard, and soon espoused Protestant beliefs. Neither did she hide her religious conversion, saving hard to buy an English-language Bible and then rooting round Derby to find someone to read it to her – a difficult task given the religious animosities of the time.

Matters became dangerous for Joan when Mary had the Catholic Mass reinstated with attendance made compulsory. Joan simply wouldn't accept this, and her refusal to attend mass attracted the attention of the local bishop, who seems to have been a particularly ardent persecutor of Protestants. During her subsequent interrogation, Joan stuck to her beliefs, denying transubstantiation and insisting that church services should be in English. This frustrated her examiners, especially as this lowly born woman knew her Bible and argued her case with fluency. Inevitably, she was condemned to death and, with her twin brother holding her hand, Joan was led to the place of execution, the Windmill Pit, a dell on the south side of the city. There she was hung over the fire with a rope to slowly burn to death, finally falling into the fire when the rope burned through.

A blue plaque remembers her sacrifice.

Address The blue plaque dedicated to Joan Wast is on the wall at the end of Lime Avenue, Derby, DE1 ITU, a cul-de-sac on the south side of the city centre; it's off the Burton Road (A5250) | Getting there The memorial is an 8-minute drive south west to Lime Avenue from Derby bus station; note that there are two Lime Avenues in Derby – so be sure to use the DE1 ITU post code | Hours Always accessible | Tip In a strange twist of religious fate, St Joseph's Catholic Church and Convent is located just a couple of hundred yards from Wast's memorial plaque.

# 56 Kedleston Hall

*Robert Adam, the Beau Brummell of interior design*

One of the region's grandest country houses, Kedleston Hall stands proud and tall amid rolling countryside, about six miles northwest of Derby. One Curzon or another has been in charge hereabouts for centuries – a Gerard Curzon arrived with William I – and even now, although the National Trust took over the Hall in the 1980s, the family have conjured themselves a private wing. Land was long the principal source of Curzon wealth, though strategic marriages and the benefits of political office were an added bonus – as was the case with Sir Nathaniel Curzon (1726–1804), the one-time MP for Derby and the man responsible for transforming the family seat.

Enterprising and rich, Nathaniel began by landscaping the grounds, making them suitably 'picturesque', with natural lakes replacing formal water features. Then he started on the house, where his plans were modified after he took a shine to Robert Adam (1728–1792), a Scottish architect and interior designer of rare ability, whose neo-classical designs were to go on to transform a platoon of country houses. Adam set to work and the north front took shape, a Palladian whopper dominated by a massive, six-columned portico. Adam was only partly responsible for the design of this section, but the more imaginative south front of 1765 was all his, its twin stone stairways sweeping down on either side of a central section resembling Constantine's triumphal arch in Rome.

Adam's interiors were meant to impress, maybe over-awe, from the grand pomposity of the Marble Hall, with its marble floor and alabaster columns, through to the Saloon with its cupola roof, and the spectacular sofas of the elaborate Blue State Drawing Room. Kedleston also possesses a collection of Indian artefacts brought back from the sub-continent by the most famous Curzon of them all, George (1859–1925), who was Viceroy of India from 1899 to 1905.

Address Kedleston Road, near Quarndon, Derby, DE22 5JH, +44 (0)1332 842191, www.nationaltrust.org.uk | Getting there Kedleston Hall is about 6 miles from Derby; there are no buses to the hall itself, but there is a bus stop a 20-minute walk away and it's reachable on several services, such as bus #114 from Derby's Albert Street | Hours Daily 11am–4pm but can vary, so check the website | Tip As far as Nathaniel Curzon was concerned, the village of Kedleston was an inconvenience, so he had it demolished, except for All Saints' Church (daily 10am–3pm, www.visitchurches.org.uk). The church is next to the Hall and it's stuffed with elaborate memorials to the Curzon family, notably the marble tomb of Lord Curzon, the Viceroy of India, and Mary, his much adored American wife.

# 57 Little John's Grave

*A giant of a man*

Legend has it that Robin Hood and his Merry Men liked to hang out in Sherwood Forest, an enormous royal woodland of oak, birch and bracken that once covered much of both Derbyshire and Nottinghamshire. Here they whiled away the hours doing what outlaws like to do – a bit of feasting here, a bit of canoodling there, not to mention a little horseplay: when Robin first met Little John, they fought with quarterstaffs (wooden staffs) for rite of passage over a timber bridge, the prelude to a long and close friendship.

In fact, Robin may not have existed at all and medieval outlaws were hardly likely to be merry. Neither is there a 'true story' of Robin's life – the earliest reference to him, in Langland's *Piers Plowman* of 1377, treats him as a fiction – but to the balladeers of 15th-century England, who invented most of Hood's folklore, this was not the point. For them, Robin was a symbol of yeoman decency, a principled opponent of evil barons, and a man who showed sympathy for the peasant, but is never credited with robbing the rich to give to the poor. The brigandage came later, as did Maid Marian, Friar Tuck *et al.*, along with a panoply of embellishments that ranged from the farcical to the feasible: King Richard I certainly didn't join Robin and Maid Marian together in marital vows, but a treacherous prioress might just conceivably have weakened Robin by excessive bleeding before his arch enemy, Red Roger, polished him off with a dagger.

Little John is supposed to have buried Robin before returning to Hathersage, the place of his birth, and it was here, with his own death approaching, that he grabbed hold of his long bow for one last time. He fired his arrow and it landed in St Michael's churchyard – and this is where his grave is today, framed by railings and suitably long (he is supposed to have been seven feet tall), but marked by a modern tombstone.

**Address** St Michael & All Angel's, Church Bank, Hathersage, Hope Valley, S32 1AJ, www.achurchnearyou.com/church/13179 | **Getting there** St Michael & All Angel's is on the edge of Hathersage, at the top of Church Bank, a short, narrow and very steep lane; Hathersage is about 38 miles from Derby and the church is roughly a mile from Hathersage railway station | **Hours** The church graveyard, where you'll find Little John's grave, is open during daylight hours; church open for visitors daily 9.30am–5.30pm | **Tip** Hathersage is an attractive little town and it's home to the enjoyable George Hotel, in the centre on Main Road (www.thegeorgehathersage.com). Pop inside the church to look at the earliest Little John tombstone – it should be in the porch.

# 58 The Lock-out Mural

*A Derby landmark: 'Workers of the world unite'?*

With every justification, Derby is proud of its industrial heritage whether through pioneering entrepreneurs like William Strutt or the workers who fought long and hard to secure better pay and conditions. A prime illustration of the latter is the bold and brightly coloured mural depicting the Silk Trades' Lock-out of 1833–34. It's painted on the outside of the Old Silk Mill pub, in the centre of town on the corner of Full Street and Sowter Road – yards from the Museum of Making. There was a pub here at the time of the lock-out, but this was demolished long ago and the present building, an attractive structure with a stone-faced ground floor and a half-timbered gable up above, dates from the 1920s.

The Silk Trades' Lock-out was a seminal moment in the UK's labour history. The 1830s were troubled times in England with mechanisation threatening both jobs and wages. Matters boiled over in Derby in late 1833, when a local silk manufacturer fired a worker for refusing to pay a fine imposed on him for shoddy workmanship. The fine was a routine ploy for keeping pay down, but this time several hundred silk workers went on strike in support of their workmate.

The strike spread up along the mills of the Derwent River Valley, loosely coordinated by a nascent union, the Grand National Consolidated Trades Union, in what was one of the first proper industrial disputes the country had ever seen. The mill owners responded by locking trade union members out of their factories and bringing in non-union labour. The state helped the owners out too, sending in extra police and troops. The strikers petitioned the mill owners: 'Our object is not to rob you, in violation of the law, but to prevent you from further robbing us… as the law permits,' but their entreaties fell on deaf ears and cold hearts – the strike ended in failure, collapsing in April 1834.

Address 19 Full Street, Derby, DE1 3AF | Getting there A 10-minute walk from Derby bus station | Hours Mural visible during daylight hours | Tip The Trades Union Congress (TUC) organises an annual Silk Mill Festival every summer; it's held on Cathedral Green (www.tuc.org.uk/events/silk-mill-festival).

# 59 Locko Park

*A country estate – and a stroll*

On the eastern peripheries of Derby, near suburban Spondon, is Locko Hall and Park, where a grand and privately owned country mansion stands neat and trim in its own parkland. The origins of the Locko estate date back to the 11th century, when the Earl of Derby granted the land to one of the lesser religious orders – the Leper Brothers of Jerusalem, aka the Lazarists. True to their name, the brothers were wont to apply strips of lint to leprous sores, hence Locko, the old French word for rags, *loques*.

After the Dissolution of the Monasteries, Locko passed to the aristocracy and then the merchant elite, including William Drury-Lowe (1753–1827), whose only daughter created a real brouhaha when she eloped to Scotland's Gretna Green, though he did forgive her promptly enough on her return. Drury-Lowe employed William Emes (1729–1803) to landscape his Locko grounds. It was a fortunate choice. A member of the Lunar Society, Emes brought Enlightenment principles to his task, creating that serene sense of space and balance, trees and lakes, found in the best of English landed estates.

The Locko grounds may be a delight, but the house itself is perhaps a tad ungainly, reflecting its numerous modifications: in 1853, for example, the Italianate bell tower was added after one of the Drury-Lowes came back from the Grand Tour determined to replicate something of what he had seen. One of the owners of the hall today is apparently a member of the Huntley and Palmer biscuit family, but free biscuits seem to be in short supply.

Locko Hall is not usually open to the public, but the park and grounds are. A bridleway scoots across the estate passing a scattering of incidental sculptures and providing handsome views of hall and lake. The stroll through the park on the bridleway includes one moderately steep hill and is just over a mile each way.

**Address** Locko Park, near Spondon, Derby, DE21 7BW, www.lockopark.co.uk | **Getting there** The most agreeable approach to Locko Park is from the south, along a country road from Spondon; you can park in the elongated lay-by close to the South Lodge entrance | **Hours** Accessible daylight hours | **Tip** From Locko Park, it's a 5-minute drive south to Bluebell Farm, Locko Road, Derby, DE21 7AR (www.bluebelldairy.co.uk), where they make their own 'artisanal' ice cream. And very tasty it is too.

# 60 Long Eaton

*Architectural niceties*

Long Eaton is a medium-sized town about 10 miles east of Derby. It's dotted with the mills that once hosted its lace-making industry, though this Lace-making slumped after World War I and since then Long Eaton has had to find other ways to feed itself – furniture-making being a case in point.

The centre of activity today is the elongated Market Place, on the north side of town, and it's here you'll find two delightful buildings designed by the architects Gorman & Ross, being the partnership of two Scots, James Gorman (1876–1920) and Clarence Rose Ross (1874–1949). The duo set themselves up here in Long Eaton in 1900 and although they didn't stay long – Ross went to Australia, Gorman to Malaya – they certainly left their mark.

First up, at 40 Market Place, is York Chambers, whose cheerful façade starts with a red sandstone ground floor set around a large horseshoe-shaped window. The door on the right sports a fancy Art Nouveau light, while up above are two handsome and contrasting sets of windows. York Chambers was originally a bank, but is now a Real Ale bar and micropub. Much of the original interior has survived, including some of the oak panelling and stained glass. Next door, 38 Market Place was also designed by Gorman & Ross and is similarly inventive, its most interesting feature being the narrow and circular brick turrets that frame the façade.

Finally, before they departed, Gorman and Ross had time to complete the distinctive Carnegie Library on Tamworth Road, a five-minute stroll from York Chambers. A single-storey structure, the library's façade is illuminated by a bright and cheerful mosaic with the figure of Learning set against a rising sun. The library is named after the steel king, Andrew Carnegie (1835–1919), who paid for hundreds of libraries to be built across the English-speaking world.

Address York Chambers, 40 Market Place, Long Eaton, Nottingham, NG10 1LT; Long Eaton Carnegie Library, Tamworth Road, Long Eaton, Nottingham, NG10 1JG | Getting there Long Eaton is 10 miles east of Derby; there are regular trains between the two, but Long Eaton Station is a good mile south of the Market Place. | Hours York Chambers: Mon 2–9pm, Tue–Thu noon–9pm, Fri & Sat noon–10pm, Sun noon–7pm; Library: Mon–Thu 9.30am–5pm, Fri 9.30am–6pm, Sat 9.30 am–2pm | Tip The Sawley Junction pub (www.sawleyjunction.co.uk), near the railway station, is a fabulous little place with a great range of Real Ales.

# 61 Mackworth Castle

*Gothic folly or delight?*

On the western peripheries of Derby, down along a country lane, stand the remains of Mackworth Castle, not actually a castle at all, but a strangely beguiling, partly ruinous, stone gatehouse without either an interior or a back wall. Considering the centre of Derby is just three miles away, it's surprising just how isolated and rural a spot this feels. No wonder then that local artists have been coming here to draw and paint the castle for decades – Frank Gresley (1855–1936) and Ernest Townsend (1880–1944) spring to mind.

It is thought that Mackworth Castle dates from the late 15th century and was intended as a sort of decorative frontispiece to a fortified manor house – of which there is no longer any trace. The two-storey 'castle' is made from local sandstone, its battlements, gargoyles, slender buttressing and mini-turrets set above and around a central arch. Decorative it may have been, but a chimney does poke nervously out of the battlements indicating that it was inhabited at one time or another.

What happened to the vanished manor house has been the subject of some debate, but it appears probable that its long demise began when the owners, the De Mackworths, were forced to sell the estate in 1655 after receiving a thumping great bill from Parliament as 'delinquents' – that is supporters of the king during the Civil War. The decaying manor house was likely put out of its misery and demolished in the 1770s, after Mackworth village passed to the influential and wealthy Mundy family. The leading Mundy – Francis Noel Clarke (1739–1815) – was a great improver of his estates and it was he who had a new farmhouse constructed behind the 'castle' plus farm labourers' cottages too. No stranger to immodesty, this particular Mundy saw himself as a great man of the Enlightenment – and, to be fair, he was indeed a patron of the artist Joseph Wright.

**Address** 59 Lower Road, Mackworth, Derby, DE22 4NF | **Getting there** From Derby Market Place, it's a 15-minute drive to Mackworth Castle via the Ashbourne Road | **Hours** Always accessible | **Tip** Mackworth's old and dignified All Saints' Church is about half a mile from the castle – keep going along the same country lane; it's currently being repaired after extensive fire damage. Samuel Richardson (1689–1761), a key figure in the evolution of the English novel, was born and baptised here in Mackworth, but was always keen to hide his rural roots.

# 62_Markeaton Park

*Derby's busiest park*

Extremely popular and recently reinvigorated, Markeaton Park occupies a large slab of land a couple of miles to the west of Derby Market Place. It was the Mundy family who bought the Manor of Markeaton in the early 16th century, passing it down through many generations until the last of them, Emily Cavendish, bequeathed the park to the city council on her death in 1929. Part of the bequest was Markeaton Hall, but this fell into disrepair when the army occupied it during World War II and it was demolished in 1964. The main buildings to survive from the Mundy era are parts of the old stables and the large brick orangery of 1775, now a tea room.

Markeaton Park was remodelled in the 18th century by a talented landscape gardener William Emes (1729–1803), but it's the park's list of extra activities that pulls in the punters today. The lake and its associated waterways allow for canoes and rowing boats, pedalos, and the mini-cascade of Markeaton Brook as first envisaged by Emes. Otherwise, the Mundy Play Centre is a particular focus with this large activity centre offering a wide variety of entertainments for toddlers and older children, including a pirate ship, bouncy castles, electric cars and mini golf.

Sports and exercise facilities include tennis courts, pitch and putt, crazy golf and an excellent and very popular BMX and skate park. Even more alluring perhaps is the Tree House Trek, a tree-top adventure located next to the Mundy Play Centre whose climbing ropes and zip-line give youngsters the chance to 'manoeuvre round obstacles, platforms and tunnels'. Supplementary attractions include a Craft Village, woodland walks, open-air theatre, a walled garden and the Famous Trains Model Railway Club, the region's largest model railway layout with over 10 different scenarios and a veritable brigade of locos and rolling stock.

Address Markeaton Lane, Derby, DE22 4AA, +44 (0)1332 640789, www.inderby.org.uk | Getting there Markeaton Park's main car park is located beside Markeaton Island, at the A38/A52 roundabout; regular buses to Markeaton Island from Full Street in the city centre | Hours Much of the park is open 24 hours, but certain sections – like the Mundy Play Centre – vary their times with the season, so check the website | Tip The park's Model Railway Club, Famous Trains, has different times from the park and charges admission – see www.famoustrains.org.uk. The main campus of Derby University is on the eastern edge of Markeaton Park and it's here you'll find its Sports Centre, which is open to students and non-students alike.

# 63 Masson Mill

*Not so dark and not so satanic*

On the edge of Matlock Bath, squeezed in tight against the River Derwent with limestone cliffs to either side, Masson Mill rambles along the side of the road, a sprawling red-brick complex dating back to the 1780s. It was the third mill of Richard Arkwright (1732–1792), whose role in the evolution of the textile industry – indeed of the entire factory system – is hard to overestimate. Arkwright was awkward and argumentative, but he was an inventor of the first order, making his first chunk of change via a waterproof dye he created for men's wigs. Later, Arkwright became interested if not obsessed by the textile industry. He set his mind to it and, in 1769, he patented the spinning frame and then its derivative, the water frame, which was designed to use the power of a waterwheel. At his first mill, in Cromford, Arkwright welded together this new machinery with a semi-skilled labour force, the two combining to turn cotton into yarn at speed. A few years later, Masson Mill was more of the same, but here the water ran a little faster.

The original Masson Mill was five storeys high, 144 feet long and 28 feet wide. The production floors were wide, open and uncluttered and the whole caboodle depended on a single waterwheel – two from 1801 – and turbines from the 1920s. The mill was extended on several occasions and the Italianate tower with its Art Deco lettering was added after the English Sewing Cotton Co. took over the mill in 1897.

Masson Mill closed in the early 1990s and is now promoted as a gateway to the Derwent Valley Mills World Heritage Site, though keeping this whopper of a building in good condition is far from easy. Inside, the highlight for the casual visitor today is the Textile Museum, where they have an extensive range of old cotton mill machinery – and a complement of guides to explain how they worked and at what speed.

**Address** 41 Derby Road, Matlock, DE4 3PY, +44 (0)1629 581001, www.massonmills.co.uk | **Getting there** Masson Mill is 17 miles north of Derby; train to either Cromford or Matlock Bath stations then a 20-minute walk | **Hours** Mon–Fri 8.30am–4pm, Sat 11am–4pm | **Tip** From Masson Mill, it's just a couple of miles to a factory shop, the excellent John Smedley Outlet, Lea Mills, Lea Bridge, Matlock, DE4 5AG (www.johnsmedley.com), where they specialise in high-quality knitwear.

# 64 Matlock

*Pass the water – spa of course*

Bisected by the River Derwent, the hilly little town of Matlock, just 20 miles north of Derby, divides into several villages – Matlock Green, Matlock Bank, and so on – though to the outsider these are largely indistinguishable, with the notable exception of Matlock Bath.

The town's name, Matlock, comes from the Old English for 'moot-oak' – a meeting place under an oak tree – but it was the thermal springs that put the place on the map rather than any ancient knees-up. A handful of Romans used the springs, but in the 18th and early 19th century visitors poured in, and today a segment of the town's main street – Dale Road just south of Derwent Way – is still flanked by a jaunty medley of Victorian and Edwardian villas that conjures the feel of a spa. The most conspicuous of these villas, The Remarkable Hare, at 77 Dale Road, has a bag of Gothic Revival features – a spiky corner turret, half-timbering, a dormer window and a miniature wooden balcony.

Victorian Matlock was famous for its hydros and their water treatments. The largest by far was Smedley's Hydro, which was opened in the 1850s. It proved a great success much to the delight of its owner, John Smedley (1803–1874), a successful textile tycoon whose own ill health and cure – probably of typhus – had convinced him of the value of hydropathy. Smedley's Hydro took over 50 years to complete, becoming in the process a rambling complex with a chunky French-style tower, a crenellated stone façade and a lavish Winter Garden, which possessed the most graceful of glass dome roofs. The hydropathy bubble burst after World War I and Smedley's Hydro was closed in the 1950s, becoming the headquarters of Derbyshire County Council, as it remains today. This means that visitors can only gaze at the exterior, though there are long-term plans to restore the hydro's fortunes by turning it into a hotel.

Address Smedley's Hydro, Derbyshire County Council, County Hall, Smedley Street, Matlock, DE4 3AG, www.derbyshire.gov.uk | Getting there Matlock is a 20-mile drive from Derby; train to Matlock station then a steep 15-minute walk uphill to County Hall | Hours Exterior always accessible | Tip On the eastern peripheries of Matlock, a narrow country road clambers up the wooded gorge that is Lumsdale Valley. It's a lovely drive and *en route* you pass the remains of several early water-driven mills, including a saw mill, a paint mill and a grinding mill. The Arkwright Society (www.cromfordmills.org.uk) is doing its best to preserve the valley.

# 65 Matlock Bath

*From spa resort to landscape delight*

Draped along the foot of a limestone gorge, Matlock Bath, 17 miles from Derby, has long been famous for its thermal springs, with the water gushing up from around 2,000 feet below ground level at a constant 20°C. Both the Celts and the Romans enjoyed the warm springs as did the Saxons, but things only began to blossom during Georgian times, when taking the waters became the fashion. It was then that the gentry repaired to Matlock Bath to drink and bathe in the mineral-rich waters, hoping to cure or at least ameliorate various ailments, from gout, arthritis and rheumatism through to skin conditions like psoriasis and eczema. At first, Matlock Bath was hard to reach, but the completion of the Cromford Canal in 1794 made things easier and a road was pushed through in the 1810s. The final piece of the transport jigsaw was the completion of the Derby, Matlock, Manchester rail line in 1849.

Matlock Bath billed itself as 'Little Switzerland', and to cater for its visitors it sprouted assembly rooms, gaming rooms, pump rooms, guest houses and hotels. The high point came with the visit of Princess, later Queen, Victoria in 1832. Her whistle-stop tour confirmed Matlock Bath as a society spa, though quite what the hard-pressed mill workers of neighbouring Cromford made of all these shenanigans is not recorded.

The spa's capacious Grand Pavilion was completed in 1910, but by then changing tastes were leading to the decline of the spa town and the rise of the seaside resort. Today, Matlock Bath's most engaging features are essentially natural and you might want to start in Derwent Gardens, where several thermal springs emerge, hence the water features and tufa stone grottoes. The nearby footbridge spans the river to reach the Lovers' Walks, a series of footpaths that negotiates the wooded slopes on that side of the gorge. And very pleasant walking it is too.

**Address** Derwent Gardens, Derby Road, Matlock, DE4 3NR, www.derbyshiredales.gov.uk | **Getting there** Derwent Gardens are beside the main road – the A6 – about 17 miles north of Derby; train to Matlock Bath station then a 10-minute walk | **Hours** Derwent Gardens are always accessible except during special events, including Matlock Bath Illuminations in Sep & Oct | **Tip** Most of Matlock's hydros are long gone, but the New Bath Hotel & Spa, New Bath Road, Matlock Bath, Matlock, DE4 3PX (www.newbathhotelandspa.com) offers a first-rate range of treatments and has an outdoor lido fed by thermal spring water.

# 66 Melbourne Hall & Gardens

*Aristocratic gardening*

Melbourne, some 12 miles south of Derby, has perhaps the quaintest town centre in the whole of Derbyshire, with the beautiful church of St Michael and St Mary standing just a few yards from Melbourne Hall, home of the impeccably aristocratic Marquess of Lothian. The Hall itself is shielded from view to its north and west by a scrabble of courtyards and outbuildings, but when you reach the gardens the house comes into full view, the fluid balances of its Georgian façade belying a convoluted architectural history. Inside, the house is comfortable rather than grand, though the Drawing Room is a picture of elegance and there is a veritable battalion of family portraits.

Behind the Hall, the gardens are nothing short of spectacular. They have several distinct areas, but a visit begins in the formal garden whose origins date back to Thomas Coke (1674–1727), Vice Chamberlain to Queen Anne and a keen gardener, whose green fingers brought him and his family within a whisker of financial ruin.

In the formal garden, there are terraces and multiple flights of steps, yew hedges that roll like green clouds (as they are supposed to), a reedy pool or two, walkways lined with shrubs, and acres of lawn. A platoon of statuettes is dotted around and about in this section. The best are the carefully crafted lead sculptures of John Nost (d.1729), a Fleming who went down a storm with the English aristocracy for his love of the Baroque, as illustrated here by his chubby cherubs and over-the-top Mercury.

Another part of the garden is devoted to a simply gorgeous flower display, but the high point is the delicate beauty of the 'Birdcage', a wrought-iron arbour of exquisite design featuring stylised acanthus, laurel and oak leaves. The ironsmith responsible was Robert Bakewell (1682–1752), who came to Coke's notice after the former moved to Melbourne – a fortunate occurrence for both.

Address Church Square, Melbourne, Derby, DE73 8EN, +44 (0)1332 862502, www.melbournehall.com | Getting there Melbourne is a 9-mile drive south of Derby; from Derby bus station catch Arriva no. 2 | Hours Opening hours for the Hall & Gardens are limited (visit the website for details) | Tip Melbourne Hall's courtyards and outbuildings hold the excellent Melbourne Hall Tea Rooms, where the scones are delicious and the service outstanding. In the same complex are several shops covering antiques, jewellery, wine and beer.

# 67 Midland War Memorial

*Lutyens parades his skills*

Within sight of the railway station, the large and striking Midland Railway War Memorial was unveiled to great civic fanfare in December 1921. The memorial was designed by Sir Edwin Lutyens (1869–1944), who had by then established an Empire-wide reputation for his skill and versatility as an architect, reconfiguring anything from country houses to castles and designing sombre, understated war memorials, the most famous of which is the Cenotaph in London. Indeed, Lutyens was a leading light of the Imperial War Graves Commission as it set about establishing clear and precise guidelines for the cemeteries it was having laid out at the end of World War I.

Here in Derby, Lutyens adopted his familiar classical style with a cenotaph (empty tomb) of Portland stone rising above its immediate surroundings. The sides of the cenotaph bear the Midland Railway's coat of arms, enclosed in a laurel wreath, and on top is the recumbent figure of the unknown soldier, partly covered by his greatcoat and with a helmet and bayonet at his feet. Lutyens kept the soldier largely hidden from view to emphasise the sense of soldierly sacrifice – he could be any one of us – and although the size of the plot is perhaps rather small for the size of the memorial, it's an effective monument all the same.

The bronze plaques attached to the stone wall at the back of the cenotaph are inscribed with the names of the company's dead. The list is long: the Midland Railway was Derby's largest employer with a local workforce of around 12,000. At the start of the war, hundreds of these workers volunteered to join the army and, by the time of the armistice, almost 3,000 of them had been killed and 7,000 wounded. The toll among the railway workers pushed the Midland into employing women as porters, conductors and guards, but the company was always chary of taking women on as train drivers.

**Address** Midland Road, Derby, DE1 2SQ | **Getting there** The Midland Railway War Memorial is yards from Derby railway station | **Hours** Always accessible | **Tip** The War Memorial backs onto the garden of the Midland Hotel, the oldest purpose-built railway station hotel in Europe. It was opened in 1841 and occupies a handsome, symmetrical building of Victorian design, though it's currently experiencing troubled times.

# 68 Museum of Making

*Factory life begins here*

Derby's main claim to historical fame is as the site of the world's first modern factory – the Silk Mill established by John and Thomas Lombe and in operation from around 1721. The Lombe brothers realised that the demand for spun silk was outstripping supply. Sensing an opportunity, John (1693–1722) went to Italy to discover why the silk spinning there was technologically ahead of that in England. His spying was successful and he returned with a bag of secrets, enabling Thomas (1685–1739) to register patents for 'three sorts of engines never before made or used in Great Britain'. Thomas was off on the road to wealth and success but not John: legend has it that the Italians were so enraged by the filching of their secrets that they dispatched an assassin who polished him off.

The Lombe Silk Mill was built on an islet in the River Derwent. It was powered by a water wheel until 1828 and steam thereafter. Production peaked in the 1830s, but declined thereafter. A partial building collapse and a fire of 1910 badly damaged the factory so the substantial brick structure visitors see today is far from original. That said, recycled 18th-century bricks were used in the rebuild and the vaguely Italianate tower as well as the smaller neighbouring tower are both pretty much identical to what went before.

It's hard to turn the yawning spaces of a former factory into an enjoyable museum, but the Museum of Making does its gallant and enterprising best. The collection spreads over three main floors with Floor 1 explaining the early industrial development of Derby and the Derwent River Valley. Floor 2 features a large model railway set-up and a display on Rolls-Royce. Here also is the 'Assemblage', a delightful pot-pourri of historical items, from railway signs and stone memorials to a retrieved length of ship's piping hit by a German bullet in World War II.

**Address** Silk Mill Lane, Derby, DE1 3AF, +44 (0)1332 641901, www.derbymuseums.org | **Getting there** A 10-minute walk from Derby bus station | **Hours** Tue–Sat 10am–5pm, Sun 10am–4pm and Bank Holiday Mondays 10am–5pm | **Tip** The museum's model railway is a splendid affair and trains are run regularly – consult www.midlandrailwaystudycentre.org.uk for times. There's also the Famous Trains model railway in Markeaton Park, by the main car park (www.famoustrains.org.uk).

# 69_ The National Forest

*From pits and quarries to wondrous woodland*

Small-town Swadlincote, about 18 miles from Derby, anchors the southern reaches of Derbyshire where a chubby finger of land pokes out between neighbouring Leicestershire and Staffordshire. For much of its history, Swadlincote's good fortune was its coal and clay, deposits that led to the collieries, brickworks and potteries that dominated the local economy from the early 19th through to the late 20th century, when things came to a juddering halt: the last colliery, Cadley Hill, closed in 1988 and most of the potteries closed shortly after.

At about the same time, perhaps to the surprise of those Derbyshire folk who had witnessed the collapse of their industries, the UK government established the National Forest Company, a not-for-profit organisation whose main aim was refreshingly clear: the planting of a National Forest over the old industrial belt that stretched across south Derbyshire and its immediate environs. It may all have seemed rather high-minded – the forest was billed as a key element in the UK's response to the 1992 Earth Summit in Rio – but, in the event, it has worked a treat with statistics that speak for themselves: almost 10 million trees have been planted since the forest was created and woodland, mostly native broadleaf, covers 25 per cent of the land, when it was once 6 per cent.

Attracting visitors to the National Forest has always been a priority and in recent years existing attractions – like Calke Abbey and Melbourne Hall – have been incorporated within a general access plan. There are also a pair of visitor centres near Swadlincote. Both provide access to a wide range of well-signed woodland walks, but whereas the Rosliston Forestry Centre is simple and straightforward, a little like a community centre, the Conkers Discovery Centre is more elaborate with all sorts of stuff for kids on both land and lake.

Address Rosliston Forestry Centre, Burton Road, Rosliston, Swadlincote, DE12 8JX, +44 (0)1283 563483, www.roslistonforestrycentre.co.uk; Conkers Discovery Centre, Rawdon Road, Swadlincote, DE12 6GA, +44 (0)1283 216633, www.visitconkers.com | Getting there From Rosliston Forestry Centre, it's about 6 miles east to Swadlincote and 20 miles northeast to Derby; from Conkers Discovery Centre, it's about 3 miles north to Swadlincote and 19 miles northeast to Derby | Hours See websites for seasonal opening hours | Tip You can help by dedicating or sponsoring a tree. Contact the National Forest Company (www.nationalforest.org), choose your dedication and make your donation. They'll do the rest. You can even visit your tree!

# 70_National Sikh Museum

*British Sikhs display their culture and history*

There are around 10,000 Sikhs in Derbyshire, half a million or so in England, and here in Derby's Pear Tree district, you'll find a modern complex comprising a Sikh temple – the Sri Guru Singh Sabha Gurdwara – and the National Sikh Museum. There are Sikh temples in every British city, so they are certainly not rare, but the museum is currently unique: its main aim is to celebrate Sikh culture and history – and what a proud history it is too.

Originating in the Punjab in the late 15th century, the Sikh religion's first leader was Guru Nanak Dev Ji (1469–1539). Thereafter, the faith became more defined with its most familiar custom being the wearing of the turban by Sikh men and women alike. Its spiritual capital became Amritsar, in the Punjab, the Sri Harmandir Sahib (Golden Temple) its holiest temple. The Sikh religion was always different from, and opposed aspects of, both Islam and Hinduism. This placed it in a precarious position and the Sikhs have long been subject to bouts of persecution. Neither has the situation improved since independence in 1947: Pakistan and India have repeatedly squabbled over the Punjab, and Sikhs have faced a constant struggle for the creation of an independent homeland.

The museum spreads over two large floors. The lower floor celebrates the key role the Sikhs played in the British Indian Army with pointers on various military campaigns and biographies of individual soldiers. Upstairs, in the Sarkar-e-Khalsa Art Gallery, a collection of devotional and historical paintings tracks through Sikh history. Here also is a model of the Golden Temple with notes on those occasions when it has been attacked. A further section deals with the bitter events of 1984 when the Indian Army attacked the Golden Temple, two Sikh bodyguards assassinated Indira Gandhi in response, and an anti-Sikh pogrom followed, continuing into the 1990s.

**Address** 149 Princes Street, Pear Tree, Derby, DE23 8NT, +44 (0)1332 402530, www.nationalsikhmuseum.com | **Getting there** A 50-minute walk from Derby Market Place; train to Pear Tree station then a 10-minute walk | **Hours** Daily 10am–3pm | **Tip** Rather surprisingly, Peartree railway station has survived and is located in one of the more obscure corners of the city. It's close to the woodlands of Ormaston Park.

# 71 Nightingale's Statue

*The 'Lady with the Lamp'*

By any standard, Florence Nightingale (1820–1910) was a remarkable woman. Born in Florence to a wealthy and well-connected family of liberal outlook, she spent her early summers at the family's home in Lea, just north of Derby. The fashion for rugged scenery made Derbyshire an appealing hidey-hole for the Nightingales, but by the time Florence was in her late teens, she was more concerned with taking medicine and food to impoverished villagers than by the scenery. In her 20s, Florence came to feel she was called by God to devote her life to the service of others and, although she delayed telling her parents, she declared her plans to commit to nursing in 1844.

It was the Crimean War (1853–1856) against Russia that made Nightingale famous. When she arrived in Istanbul, conditions at the British military hospital were dire: medicines were scarce, hygiene was neglected and mass infections common. Nightingale, who had influential contacts back home, brought pressure to bear and slowly transformed the situation, reducing the death rate from 42 per cent to 2 per cent – a great achievement – and a much-lionised Florence became an icon of the age with paintings and poems celebrating her wandering hospital wards as the 'Lady with the Lamp'.

After her return to England, Florence spent much of the rest of her life laying the foundations of modern, professional nursing – no wonder, then, that all sorts of things were named after her. In Derby, the most interesting memorial is this delightful statue of her on London Road, beside what was formerly the Derbyshire Royal Infirmary. Plonked on a pedestal and carrying a lamp aloft, Florence is depicted as a youngish woman of determined demeanour. It was the work of an aristocratic sculptor, Lady Feodora Gleichen, who underestimated the skills of the local population in detaching the lamp – something of a regular occurrence.

Address London Road, just north of its junction with Liversage Road, Derby, DE1 2BP | Getting there A 12-minute walk from Derby bus station | Hours Always accessible | Tip The old Derbyshire Royal Infirmary behind the Nightingale statue closed in 2009. Since then, new homes have replaced what was there before, but some features of the Victorian hospital have been preserved, principally two striking mini-façades with pepper-pot towers; one of them contains the smart Pepperpot Restaurant (www.pepperpotderby.co.uk).

# 72 Norbury

*An English country church*

The scattered hamlet of Norbury trails along country lanes just to the south of the River Dove, where it marks the boundary between Derbyshire and Staffordshire. Mentioned in the Domesday Book, Norbury was gifted to one of William the Conqueror's followers before being passed to the Fitzherberts, an extensive clan who ruled the local roost for several centuries. The family were noted Catholics, which brought them heaps of trouble in the 16th century, but the name is perhaps most frequently recalled with reference to Mrs Fitzherbert (1756–1837), the secret and illegal wife of George IV.

The church of St Mary and St Barlok's, at the heart of Norbury, looks out over a graveyard of slate tombs and ancient yew trees. It's an exquisite scene, though the church is of an unusual design, the clock and bell tower rising in the middle above the porch. Inside, the Fitzherberts have left a set of beautifully carved tomb-chests and some fine medieval stained glass. Next door, the old Manor House, with its long brick façade and mullion windows, mostly dates from the 17th century and is now owned and rented out by the National Trust.

Here in Norbury as elsewhere, generations of ordinary villagers came and went with barely a mention, but for once the historical fog lifts in the strange case of Ann Moore (1761–1813). Born here, the daughter of a day-labourer, Ann had reached her forties when she claimed that she had not eaten any solid food for five years and had not drunk any liquid for four. Moore's story appeared in newspapers and medical journals, and her house in Tutbury, 13 miles from Norbury, became the site of a sort of freak show pilgrimage, with crowds turning up to watch her and many leaving donations. This pantomime lasted for several years until the fraud was discovered – her daughter had smuggled her food to her – whereupon Ann upped sticks and disappeared.

Address St Mary and St Barlok's Church, off the B5033, Norbury, Ashbourne, DE6 2ED | Getting there The church is at the end of a short lane signed from the B5033, about 5 miles from Ashbourne | Hours The church is usually open daily from about 10am–3pm; the Manor House and gardens are open May–Sep Thu 10.30am–2.30pm (www.nationaltrust.org.uk) | Tip The best approach to Norbury is from the north with the road scuttling through the pretty little village of Ellastone before crossing the River Dove over a double-span stone bridge that dates back to the 18th century.

# 73 Nottingham Road Cemetery

*Dead and often forgotten*

In 1853, the Derby Burial Board was established to solve a problem – what to do with the dead of a fast-growing town when the existing graveyards were filling up. The Board didn't hang about, taking just a few months to create a municipal cemetery on an undulating slab of land between Nottingham Road (then the main road east out of town) and the Derby Canal (which has since been filled in). Warming to its task, the Board had the Bishop of Lichfield consecrate the burial ground in early 1855 – well most of it: one part was left unconsecrated for Catholics, atheists and assorted sectarians.

For planting and landscaping, the board sought the advice of William Barron (1805–1891), the head gardener of Elvaston Castle. His speciality – apart from topiary – was the planting of evergreens and mature trees, notably beech, weeping ash and Turkey oak. Some of Barron's trees survive today, but they have been supplemented by trees from later efforts and, most recently, by a large-scale bulb planting. For the design of the cemetery's main entrance, the board chose a local architect, Henry Isaac Stevens (1806–1873). Stevens banged out neo-Gothic churches as if there were no tomorrow, but here he was a tad more adventurous, composing a suitably sombre, stone gatehouse whose clock tower rises above an arched carriageway, flanked by a screen of lodges and chapels.

Footpaths thread their way across the cemetery, which is dotted with those memorials so beloved of the Victorians: angels stand guard over some graves, others are surmounted by a broken pillar garlanded with a laurel wreath – 'Victory in death' – and yet others are topped by a draped urn, the return of the body to ashes. Here also is a distinctive Portland stone Cross of Sacrifice, the standard signifier of a Commonwealth War Cemetery; 40 servicemen from both world wars are buried near the Cross.

Address Nottingham Road Cemetery, Nottingham Road, Chaddesden, Derby, DE21 6FN, www.derby.gov.uk | Getting there A 10-minute drive east from central Derby; bus 24, 26 and Indigo | Hours Summer daily 9am–7.30pm, winter daily 9am–4.30pm | Tip Since it was opened, the cemetery has been extended on several occasions with 'Nottingham Road New Cemetery' now located directly across Nottingham Road to the north. One grave to look out for is that of Abel Boden, an engine driver on the Midland Railway, who composed his own epitaph in verse – 'My valves are all thrown open…'

# 74 Ockbrook Moravian Church

*Surprise, surprise – Moravians in rural Derbyshire*

Intolerance and religious persecution have a habit of washing people up where you least expect them – and the Moravian Settlement in the village of Ockbrook, six miles east of Derby, is a case in point. The Moravians were an early Protestant sect originating in what is today the Czech Republic. Pre-dating Luther by about 50 years, they attacked the Catholic church for its corruption – the sale of indulgences being high up on their list – and a raft of its religious practices. In time, the Moravians came to dominate religion in their homeland, but when the full force of the Habsburg Counter-Reformation fell upon them, their situation was transformed: some hid their beliefs, others were martyred, and yet others fled into exile.

In the 1720s, Nicolaus Zinzendorf (1700–1760), the Count of Saxony, provided sanctuary to a group of refugee Moravians. Zinzendorf was an evangelical Christian and his involvement with those under his protection seems to have ignited a religious revival. Now, the desire to evangelise and establish new Moravian communities became unstoppable with one result being the purchase of six acres here in Ockbrook in around 1750.

Initially, the newcomers found it hard going, but in time they established a pious, hard-working community built on prayer and worship. The heart of the community was a sequence of red-brick buildings flanking a main street they called The Settlement. The three key buildings – the school, the manse (at no.10) and the church – have survived in fine fettle, but it's the church that catches the eye, a singularly pretty affair approached up a tree-lined path. The church façade is classically Georgian and comes complete with a wooden cupola and a clock by John Whitehurst. Be sure to pop into the church if it's open.

Address Ockbrook Moravian Church, 12 The Settlement, Ockbrook, Derby, DE72 3RJ, +44 (0)1332 405202, www.ockbrook.moravianchurch.uk | Getting there A 15-minute drive east from Derby Market Place; bus 9A and 9C | Hours Church opening hours are variable, but there is a service every Sunday at 11am | Tip Ockbrook is just off the A52, the busy dual carriageway connecting Derby and Nottingham. The road has been named the Brian Clough Way after the famous football manager.

# 75 The Pentrich Revolt

*E. P. Thompson 'A wholly proletarian insurrection'*

Like much of the rest of Derbyshire, tiny Pentrich, some 13 miles north of Derby, was transformed by the Industrial Revolution with its coal and iron mined, its engineering works founded and textile mills built. There was also hardship, especially after the end of the Napoleonic Wars in 1815, when commodity prices rose just as the demand for manufactured goods slumped. As conditions worsened, so rumours of riot and insurrection spread – and the authorities were nervous: they had the French Revolution at the back of their minds.

The events of what is often coined 'the Last Revolution in England' took place in and around Pentrich on 9 and 10 June, 1817, though 'Revolution' is something of a misnomer for a sad tale of poorly informed working folk gulled by a government agent. The bald facts are these: on Sunday 8 June the 'rebels' met at the White Horse Inn in Pentrich, where they had heard that revolutionaries were gathering all over the country (they weren't). Encouraged, they decided to march on Nottingham, starting the next day. On the march, there were a few minor incidents involving individual house owners, but at Eastwood they were confronted by a detachment of dragoons and promptly ran for it.

The Derby trial that followed was for retribution not justice: 3 were executed, 14 transported and 80 others imprisoned, while the judge ranted that 'Your object was to wade through the blood of your countrymen'. At the trial, the prosecution also avoided having any mention made of William Oliver, the police informer who played a key role in stirring up the marchers in the first place.

Nowadays, Pentrich makes the most of its revolutionary heritage with plaques recording its various events all over the place. One of the more surprising is the plaque outside St Matthew's Church, which notes that the curate here hid rebels from government troops.

**Address** Main Road, Pentrich, Ripley DE5 3RE | **Getting there** Pentrich is 13 miles from Derby on the B6013 | **Hours** Plaques always accessible | **Tip** Percy Bysshe Shelley wrote the pamphlet *We Pity the Plumage, But Forget the Dying Bird* (1817) contrasting the wretched fate of the 'Pentrich Martyrs' with the public mourning for the death of Princess Charlotte in childbirth a day earlier. For more on the course of the revolt, pop into The Dog at Pentrich, where they have a series of information boards.

# 76 Pickford's House & Museum

*A most inventive architect*

Ambitious and enterprising, the architect Joseph Pickford (1734–1782) moved to Derby in 1760 and soon slipped into gentrified company, counting the painter Joseph Wright and the clockmaker John Whitehurst among his many friends. Pickford picked up work designing houses in the Palladian style for his wealthier contacts, sometimes in Derby – St Helen's House is the prime example – but mostly in rural Derbyshire.

In the late 1760s, Pickford bought himself several plots of land on Friar Gate and it was here, at number 41, that he built what is now known as Pickford's House. Pickford wanted his new build to showcase his skills, so he made sure its grand Georgian façade outdid its neighbours: look out for the recessed central bay with its stylish stone trim, the Roman-style doorcase, and the Greek urns on the balustrade.

The house has been a municipal museum since the 1980s and has a certain jumbled charm, the best sections dealing with Pickford's life and times. Visitors are advised to start on the top floor, which holds a fascinating collection of toy theatres, many of which are extraordinarily elaborate. Down below is a real mixture – an Edwardian bathroom, a 1940s bedroom, an 1820s kitchen – but the highlight is the Dining Room with its pair of Joseph Wright portraits and splendid chimney piece of Carrara marble decorated with Blue John inserts.

Pickford carefully engineered the Dining Room to be bigger than normal by raising the ceiling. Here, the family held evening entertainments – or 'routs' – with food, music and dancing, a custom continued by Mary Pickford after her husband's demise. These attempts at sociability were not, however, universally admired, with a very grumpy usher from Repton School complaining of 'beau wits and giggling belles … with noise and nonsense clattering round the board'.

Address 41 Friar Gate, Derby, DE1 1DA, +44 (0)1332 641901, www.derbymuseums.org | Getting there A 15-minute walk from Derby bus station | Hours Tue–Sat 10am–5pm | Tip The handsome Georgian façade of the Pickford House is matched by its neighbours. Here, Pickford was responsible for 44 Friar Gate, which is distinguished by its elaborate ground-floor windows and first-floor blind arcade. The property is currently occupied by Chevin Homes.

# 77 Pleasley Pit

*King Coal – colliers and collieries*

The Derbyshire Coalfield stretched right along the east side of the county, from Chesterfield to Swadlincote. When the coal industry was nationalised in 1947, there were 68 Derbyshire collieries and in 1954 the workforce was tallied at 36,000 men. In the next decades, the industry contracted until, when the Miners' Strike began in 1984, there were just 13,500 Derbyshire pitmen left. For a variety of reasons, support for the strike was strong in the north of the county and weak in the south, but if those who continued working thought Thatcher's Conservatives would reward them by not closing their pits, they were mistaken; the county's last collieries closed in 1993.

Considering how important the pits were to Derbyshire, there are surprisingly few visible reminders of the coal industry: the slag heaps have been grassed over and most of the pit heads are long gone. The main exception is Pleasley Pit, where much of the infrastructure has survived – somewhat by accident at first, but more recently thanks to the efforts of a group of volunteers. Pleasley began cutting coal in the 1870s, but in 1983 the Coal Board rationalised production with the neighbouring Shirebrook Colliery taking precedence. Thereafter, much of Pleasley's surface infrastructure was demolished, but much was left alone, including the two headstocks, one of the 40-metre-high (131 feet) brick chimneys, and the engine-house complex, containing the two vintage steam winders that were used to raise the coal.

It's only on a guided tour that the massive industrial equipment that surrounds visitors makes much sense: with a flick of a button, the track that the coal wagons took springs into life and you can observe the steam winders in action or see how helmet lights evolved. Many of the guides are ex-miners and visiting Pleasley was, for this author, one of the highlights of writing this book.

**Address** Pleasley Pit Visitor Centre & Mining Museum, Pleasley Pit, Pit Lane, Pleasley, Mansfield, NG19 7PH, +44 (0)1623 818928, www.pleasleypittrust.org.uk | **Getting there** About 27 miles north of Derby; buses from Chesterfield to Pit Lane, about half a mile from Pleasley Pit | **Hours** Visitor Centre open daily except Tue 9.30am–2pm; Museum open Wed & Thu 10am–1pm, Sun 10am–1.30pm | **Tip** From Pleasley, it's just 5 miles north to another former coal mining community, Bolsover, where pride of place goes to Bolsover Castle, a sprawling affair mostly dating from the 17th century and with a grand indoor Riding House (www.english-heritage.org.uk).

# 78 Pride Park Stadium

*Pride comes before a fall*

In 1991, Derby's Lionel Victor Pickering (1931–2006), who had made a fortune from free local newspapers, became the majority shareholder of Derby County Football Club, aka The Rams. He purchased his holding from Robert Maxwell, the infamous newspaper magnate, shortly before his death – Maxwell being far from the only disreputable figure to get their claws into and onto the club. The Pickering regime worked well: he invested heavily, bringing in good players and a sound manager, Jim Smith, who secured promotion to the Premiership in 1996.

Neither were Pickering's ambitions limited to the team. Aware of the limitations of the Baseball Ground, he wanted to build a swanky new stadium, escaping the cramped Victorian terraces of the Pear Tree district for the wide – well wider – spaces of what had been the old railyards near the city centre. At the time, the move of football clubs to new, all-seater stadiums was in its infancy, but Middlesbrough's Riverside Stadium had just been completed, so Pickering hired the same architects, the Miller Partnership, who kept to the same basic design.

The new stadium was ready for the start of the 1997–98 season. Many fans loved it and it's true that the bowl-shaped design improved the view of the pitch from the stands, but its business-park surroundings were uninspiring. The stadium had a capacity of just over 33,000, an increase on its predecessor, which should have helped secure Derby's future, but in 2002 the club was relegated and hit the skids. This ended the Pickering era, but the financial shenanigans that followed were even worse and the club has been bobbing around the lower divisions pretty much ever since, though matters do seem at last to be improving.

A conspicuous statue of Brian Clough and Peter Taylor stands outside the ground as a reminder of more successful times. Hopefully, they will return.

**Address** Pride Park Stadium, Derby, DE24 8XL, +44 (0)1332 821082, www.dcfc.co.uk | **Getting there** A 20-minute walk east of Derby railway station | **Hours** For details of Derby County football matches, see www.dcfc.co.uk | **Tip** Just a couple of hundred yards from Pride Park Stadium is the distinctive-looking Derby Arena (www.derbyarena.co.uk), a multi-use, state-of-the-art, indoor sports arena and velodrome.

# 79_Primark

*Their first UK store*

In late September 1974, Hughie Green, the presenter of TV's *Opportunity Knocks* and one of the country's biggest stars, was on Babington Lane in Derby to open the UK's first Primark store. As Hughie expected, a large crowd gathered to gaze at him and among them was the man who had footed the bill, Arthur Ryan (1935–2019), Primark's founder, chairman and CEO. A perceptive and hard-working Irishman, Ryan had started the company – originally known as Penneys – five years before in Dublin with the support of the Westons, one of Ireland's richest and most powerful families.

Ryan's major insight was that offering 'amazing fashion, at amazing prices' for the under-35 market would be a huge hit – and he was proved right, perhaps beyond his wildest dreams. Part of Ryan's strategy was to strip out everything that was unnecessary – as he put it himself: 'No gimmicks. You like it or you don't. And they'll tell us soon enough. If we don't like it, we get rid of it. We don't have annual sales because we don't hang around waiting for January if we get a problem in October.' Armed with Ryan's tough intelligence, Primark expanded rapidly after Derby, with the purchase of 40 prime-site Littlewoods stores in 2005, giving the company the major boost it was by then ready for. In Derby, Primark moved to larger premises on the Corn Market in 2008.

Today, Primark has stores in 17 countries and employs more than 80,000 people in Europe and the USA. As with any major retailer, the company has been heavily criticised for aspects of its business model, notably for alleged child and forced labour in its supply chain, but the company has proved adept at rising to these challenges. On the other hand, there can be no doubt that Primark has fuelled the trend for fast fashion in which consumers buy heaps of items at prices that make them effectively discardable. Some people may deplore this, but the queues at Primark just get longer.

Address Primark, 28–31 Corn Market, Derby, DE1 2DG, +44 (0)1332 297209, www.primark.com | Getting there A 7-minute walk from Derby bus station | Hours Mon–Wed 9am–6pm, Thu–Sat 9am–7pm, Sun 10.30am–4.30pm | Tip Derby's Primark is footsteps from the revived Market Hall, where one of the best food stalls is undoubtedly Colombo Street (Sri Lankan).

# 80 Railway Terrace

*The home of Midland Railway*

In the space of a decade, Victorian Derby became a major rail centre with a splendid station, the Trijunct Station, named after the three rail companies that initially shared its facilities. Workshops, shunting yards and engine sheds followed, but although the city was – and still is – a major force in Britain's railway industry, it didn't save the original Derby railway station from either the Luftwaffe or the developers. Happily, in the last few years there has been an imaginative refit and redesign and this has improved matters considerably.

In the 1840s, the Midland Railway outmanoeuvred its rivals, becoming the town's largest employer – until the company was itself swallowed up by a rival in the 1920s. The Midland left its architectural footprint on Derby, nowhere more so than on Railway Terrace, which extends north from today's railway station. Here you'll find the elongated façade of the Midland Railway Institute, whose elegant red-brick and terracotta symmetries culminate in an octagonal corner turret with copper-green roof and cupola. In the full flush of industrial paternalism, the Institute was established as a cultural and educational centre for railway workers in 1892 – and the interior came complete with a splendid ballroom.

Continuing north along Railway Terrace, former Midland Railway offices line up along the right-hand side of the road while the left is taken up by what were once railway workers' cottages, neat and trim, two-storey terrace houses whose paired doorways have stone lintels and pillars. The terraces, which include an excellent traditional pub and microbrewery – the Brunswick Inn – date from 1842. They were designed by Francis Thompson (1808–1895), who had a stellar career as a railway architect, planning Derby's Trijunct Station as well as 13 other stations, most of which are unfortunately long gone.

Address Railway Terrace, Derby, DE1 2RU | Getting there Railway Terrace is next to Derby railway station | Hours Always accessible | Tip Railway Terrace is on the west side of Derby railway station, while the Derby Railway Roundhouse is on the east. Ask and you will be allowed to walk from one side of the station to the other, over the footbridge spanning the train lines.

# 81 Reg Parnell Memorial

*The Derby speedster*

The Derby to Nottingham corridor is famous for its concentration of mechanics and engineers – one of the reasons why Rolls-Royce has stayed here and Toyota was so easily tempted. In the 1920s and 1930s, many a mechanic made a beeline for the Royal Standard pub, beside the Exeter Bridge, on account of its being run by the Parnells, who were legendary hereabouts as motor engine people. The family's big success story was Reg Parnell (1911–1964), who, in 1935, bought his first racing car – an old two-litre Bugatti single-seater – determined to become a champion racing driver.

Things went well at first, but in 1937 Reg's career suffered a major setback when he crashed into – and severely injured – a female racing driver, a certain Kay Petre (1903–1994), who never raced competitively again. Reg had his racing licence revoked for two years, but it was during the ban that he tried his hand at car dealing and team management, at both of which he proved adept.

After the ban had run its course, Reg clocked up all sorts of firsts, most notably taking part in the inaugural World Championship Formula One race at Silverstone. These pioneering times favoured ingenuity as Reg demonstrated at the 1947 Swedish Grand Prix. In between races, Parnell had fitted twin rear wheels to his vehicle to improve its road-holding on the ice. His opponents objected but Reg had checked the rulebook and it didn't cover this particular eventuality. Sadly, Reg died young, following an appendix operation, and his motoring interests passed to his son, Tim (1932–2017). Like his dad, Tim stayed loyal to Derby and both are buried in All Saints Churchyard, Findern, Derbyshire.

As for the Royal Standard, the Parnells have moved on – though Reg is recalled by a commemorative plaque – and nowadays the pub sells a good range of real ales in well-kept premises dating back to the 1860s.

**Address** The Royal Standard, 1 Derwent Street, Derby, DE1 2ED, +44 (0)1332 200074, www.royalstandardderby.co.uk | **Getting there** A 7-minute walk from Derby bus station | **Hours** Mon & Tue 4–11pm, Wed 3–11pm, Thu–Sat noon–11pm, Sun noon–6pm | **Tip** Drinkers are spoilt for choice near the Council House with the traditional Exeter Arms (www.exeterarms.co.uk), near the Royal Standard on Exeter Place, offering 'the charm of a rural pub in the urban sprawl of Derby city centre'.

# 82 Repton Vikings

*Fear and loathing in Repton*

The well-heeled village of Repton, about 10 miles southwest of Derby, looks quiet and unruffled today, but from the 7th to the 9th century it witnessed high times as the capital of the Anglo-Saxon kingdom of Mercia. When things were going well for Mercia, so Repton prospered, but the town sat tight against the River Trent, which was a simply terrifying place to be when the Vikings of the Great Heathen Army were on the loose in the 870s. This large force, an amalgamation of different bands totalling around 4,000 men, attacked the Anglo-Saxon kingdoms in turn until, in A.D. 873, they invaded Mercia, marauding as they went before overwintering in Repton.

Perhaps surprisingly, archaeologists only investigated the Vikings' winter camp here at Repton thoroughly in the 1970s and 1980s. The team, under the leadership of Martin and Birthe Biddle, found that the raiders had dug a D-shaped enclosing ditch in what was later to become the graveyard of the church of St Wystan. At the back of the D, the church itself became the Vikings' fortified gatehouse after it had been looted. The Biddles also investigated a shallow burial mound nearby in the vicarage garden. The mound held the assorted remains of 249 individuals, but there was no agreement as to whether this was the tomb of a war lord and his retinue or the bones of Viking battle dead collected together from the Repton area. The Vikings stayed in Repton for a year, after which the church of St Wystan resumed its Christian duties.

If you're visiting Repton today, you will find the River Trent has moved north away from the village, while the trenches dug by the archaeologists have been filled in. You can, however, visit St Wystan and clamber down a narrow flight of stone steps to the crypt with its candy-twist columns. Remarkably, the crypt pre-dates the Vikings and was a royal Mercian mausoleum, though the tombs of kings Ethelbald and Ethelbert are long gone.

Address St Wystan's Church, 7 Willington Road, Repton, Derby, DE65 6FH, +44 (0)1283 619686, www.reptonchurch.uk | Getting there Repton is a 10-mile drive from Derby | Hours St Wystan's Church is normally open daily, but check the website for seasonal opening hours | Tip There are several good places to eat on Repton High Street with one of the better options being The Bull's Head (www.thebullshead.co.uk).

# 83_The Ritz Cinema, Belper

*Great cinema; great films*

The inhabitants of Belper, about nine miles north of Derby, seem to be an especially inventive lot. This small town, with a population of just 22,000, started out making nails, then turned to textiles and then, when this fizzled out, a certain Audley Williamson (1916–2004) turned up with a gloopy substance for conditioning silk stockings. Nylon stockings came into their own after World War II and seemed to scupper this business, but the gloop turned out to be great for cleaning hands – and Swarfega was born and remains popular to this day.

Swarfega may have stayed pretty much the same, but Belper has changed dramatically in recent years, turning itself from an industrial town into one with a distinctly artsy and alternative edge. Strolling along the main drag, King Street, with its cafés and shops, is now a real pleasure and it's here you'll find the Ritz Cinema, very much a community hub and key to the town's reinvention and reinvigoration.

Opened in 2006, the Ritz is housed within a creatively refurbished Victorian building, which started out as a public hall built for gatherings and events in 1882. There's just one screen – with comfortable seats and sofas – but the Ritz rustles up an especially dynamic and enterprising schedule of films, from mainstream and cult through to art house and independents. They also do a great line in 'Event Cinema', with live feeds from major theatres – at time of writing this included the showing of London National Theatre's *A Streetcar Named Desire* starring Gillian Anderson.

And then there's the Joel and Ethan Coen connection. A few years ago, the Ritz held its own spoof award ceremony 'The Ritzy' and the brothers were among the first winners. They saw the joke when they heard the news and Ethan sent a 'gracious and funny acceptance email'; there have been occasional and very friendly contacts ever since.

**Address** Ritz Cinema, 76b King Street, Belper, DE56 1QA, +44 (0)1773 822224, www.ritz-belper.co.uk | **Getting there** It's about 9 miles by car from Belper to Derby; hourly trains from Derby to Belper take about 10 minutes, then an 8-minute walk | **Hours** For show times, go to www.ritz-belper.co.uk | **Tip** A rail line cuts through the heart of Belper, running along a steep cutting with stone retaining walls. Pevsner called this a 'spectacular monument' to the Victorian railway builders, and you can observe it to good advantage from Midland View, a narrow street off King Street.

# 84 Rolls-Royce Centre

*Probably the finest aero engines in the world*

On Wednesday 4 May, 1904, Frederick Henry Royce (1863–1933) met Charles Stewart Rolls (1877–1910) at the Midland Hotel in Manchester. It was an historic meeting and one that was to have a profound effect on Derby. Over the tea and hobnobs, they agreed to form an automobile company and this was formalised as Rolls-Royce Limited two years later: Royce, the supreme mechanic, provided the technical expertise, Rolls, the financial backing and business expertise.

The first Rolls-Royces were very well received, so the company needed a car-making factory pronto. It was then that Derby City Council, with its ear close to the engineering ground, tempted them with cheap electricity and, in 1908, Rolls-Royce opened a car plant on Derby's Nightingale Road. The first Rolls-Royce, the Silver Ghost – the 'greatest car in the world' according to *Autocar* – went on sale the same year. Rolls-Royce was to operate on the Nightingale Road site until 2007, but other things changed and changed frequently, beginning with the involvement of Rolls. By 1909, he had begun to lose interest in automobiles, turning instead to aviation; it was an enthusiasm that was to kill him when the tail snapped off his plane.

Since those early days, Rolls-Royce has been nationalised and privatised, broken up and reassembled, but it has secured – in the process – a world-beating reputation for the quality of its military and civilian aircraft engines. Today, the company employs about 17,000 people in Derby, working at several sites, including a nuclear submarines research section and an aero-engine testing plant. At the Rolls-Royce Heritage Centre, part of the Learning and Development Centre, visitors can track the evolution of the Rolls-Royce aero engine from World War I onwards with around 30 engines on display – something of a specialist interest perhaps, but still intriguing.

Address Rolls-Royce Learning and Development Centre, Gate 5A, Wilmore Road, Derby, DE24 9BD, +44 (0)1332 661461, www.iaeg.com | Getting there A 10-minute drive south of Derby Market Place | Hours Tours need to be booked a minimum of three weeks ahead of time via www.rolls-royce.com/about/heritage-trust | Tip Derby is dotted with all things Rolls-Royce, but easily the most appealing building is the Art Deco Marble Hall, the company's former office block on Nightingale Road.

# 85 Roman Derby

*Hear the bark of a Roman centurion – maybe not*

In A.D. 42, there was trouble in southeast England following the death of King Cunobelin, Shakespeare's Cymbeline. One man keen to take advantage was the Emperor Claudius, who had become mightily irritated by anti-Roman collaboration between the British Celts and their French cousins. The following year, Claudius launched his invasion, landing a substantial army in Kent. It was joined by a menagerie of elephants and camels for its major battles and, by A.D. 47, the Romans had reached southern Derbyshire, where they overcame two of the more tractable of the Celtic tribes, the Cornovii and the Corieltauvi; both were agricultural peoples with few strongly defended sites.

In around A.D. 50, the Romans built a fort near the west bank of the River Derwent, but a few years later this was abandoned in favour of a stockade near the east bank in a part of Derby now known as Little Chester. The Romans called this second, river-guarding fort Derventio and paved roads ran from here to several points of the compass, including the lead-mining areas of northern Derbyshire. In time, a Celtic settlement grew up hereabouts and this is where archaeologists have discovered a miscellany of finds, most notably pottery. The settlement did not, however, outlive the collapse of Roman rule.

Some Roman remains from Derventio are on display in Derby Museum & Art Gallery, but otherwise you are going to need a lot of imagination to hear the tramp of the legionnaire's sandal on the streets of Little Chester. The one place to aim for is pedestrianised Marcus Street, a pleasant little enclave of terraced housing where the remains of a 3rd-century Roman well and a scattering of stone foundation posts were discovered in 1924. The well, which is grilled, won't take your breath away, and the interpretation board is a bit battered, but there again you won't be jostled by hordes of tourists.

Address Marcus Street, Little Chester, Derby, DE1 3SE | Getting there A 20-minute walk north of Derby Market Place | Hours The well is always visible during daylight hours, but it is outside a private residence, so please be mindful of homeowner's privacy | Tip It's a pleasant stroll south along Marcus Street to the leafy expanse of Chester Green, whose western boundary is overlooked by a seemingly endless brick wall – a wall that was part of Haslam's Foundry until it closed in 2004.

# 86 Royal Crown Derby

*Some of the fanciest porcelain ever produced*

As Derby's industrial fortunes waxed in the middle of the 18th century, so it attracted a brigade of inventive entrepreneurs, one of whom was Staffordshire's William Duesbury (1725–1786), who, in the 1750s, co-founded the first porcelain works here in the city. His main ally was Andrew Planché (1727–1805), a talented potter, whose delicate and finely executed pieces were much admired.

As it turned out, Planché didn't hang around long, but Duesbury did, improving the quality of the company's products by experimenting with different materials – soapstone and powdered glass for instance – and by employing the brightest and the best to model and paint the porcelain. His son, also William Duesbury (1763–1796), continued in the same vein and the company became a major manufacturer of colourful dinner services and fanciful figurines. There was more reward for the younger Duesbury and his successor, Robert Bloor (d. 1828), when the Prince Regent (1762–1830), that most extravagant of royals, took a shine to what was known as 'Derby Porcelain' until 1773, and 'Crown Derby' thereafter, populating several of his houses with prime Derby pieces.

Crown Derby reached the peak of its popularity in the late 19th century, its lavish and romantic designs very much in keeping with the spirit of the times; from 1890, it was also able to add the 'Royal' appellation after its appointment as 'Manufacturers of porcelain to Her Majesty'.

Since its Victorian salad days, the company has had as many downs as ups and, after much coming and going, it's now owned by the ceramic manufacturer Steelite International. Royal Crown Derby's factory is in the city centre, on Osmaston Road, but there are currently no factory tours and neither the gift shop nor the museum is open; hopefully things will change at some point as the museum holds an exemplary collection of Royal Crown Derby pieces.

Address 194 Osmaston Road, Derby, DE23 8JZ, +44 (0)1332 712800, www.royalcrownderby.co.uk | Getting there A 10-minute walk from Derby railway station | Hours Factory currently viewable from the outside only, but you can view their products, both old and new, online | Tip Derby Museum and Art Gallery has an excellent Royal Crown Derby collection, including pieces by one of the company's co-founders, Andrew Planché.

# 87_Royal School for the Deaf

*Specialist schooling at its best*

Born in Heanor, not far from Derby, William Robert Roe (1849–1920) was one of those exemplary Victorian philanthropists who did much to change the world for the better. As a young man, Roe had run a successful business as a harness maker, but his life took a dramatic turn after – though there are several versions of the tale – he witnessed a young deaf lad by the name of Jack being badly bullied. The more Roe learnt about Jack, the more offended he became at the social and educational exclusion of the deaf, and he resolved to do something about it, ultimately embarking on an international tour to raise awareness and funds.

After his return, Roe gathered together a group of like-minded philanthropists and the end result was the founding, in 1894, of what was to become the Royal School for the Deaf Derby. Roe was the school's first headteacher and he was to be succeeded by his son, William Carey (1887–1956). Very much to his credit, the first Roe was a champion of the teaching of sign language alongside finger spelling – the 'manual system' – at a time when it was the 'oral system' (teaching children to articulate and lip read) that ruled the roost. The 'oral system' was to remain dominant for many more years, but finally British Sign Language (BSL) was officially recognised as a language by the UK government in 2003.

In 1972, the school moved from its city-centre premises to a campus on the western edge of Derby. This is where it remains today as, to quote its prospectus, 'a unique provider of day and residential placements for deaf children and young people from a national catchment'. Its most recent Ofsted report was glowing in its comments, declaring that the school is where 'inspirational deaf and hearing staff inspire pupils to believe they can achieve anything. Consequently, pupils develop pride in their deaf identity and culture'.

**Address** 180 Ashbourne Road, Derby, DE22 3BH, +44 (0)1332 362512, www.rsdd.org.uk | **Getting there** The Royal School for the Deaf Derby is about 2 miles west of the city centre, off the A38; bus 2 and L2 | **Hours** Exterior always viewable but no public access – except for events and on special occasions (see their website) | **Tip** From the Royal School, it's a 10-minute walk to the Britannia Mill, Mackworth Road, a good-looking, brown-brick structure of 1912 that has been re-purposed and is now part of Derby University.

# 88 Sadler Gate

*Walk the town – and BPM Records*

Running east to west in the city centre, pedestrianised Sadler Gate is one of Derby's liveliest streets, its medley of old brick façades accommodating hairdressers, tattooists, bars and cafés. For the most part at least, modern planners have been kept at bay here and so the pattern of lanes and courtyards cutting off Sadler Gate is reminiscent of Victorian Derby, which makes for a pleasant change.

The first building of any real consequence is the Old Bell Hotel, where the recently renovated, half-timbered façade flanks and frames an exceptionally ornate doorway. The date of the Old Bell's construction is far from clear, but it does appear to be around 1650 and it certainly remained an important coaching inn for many years, while also hosting, at one time or another, stables, a doctor's surgery, a courtroom and some rudimentary holding cells.

Close by, further along the street, the hairdressers at number 48 features a particularly fanciful doorway dating to 1675, while the unassuming, three-storey façade of 'Warhammer', at number 42, has reddish brick up top and a slender Georgian doorway to the side. Footsteps away, an alley on the north side of Sadler Gate opens out into the Old Blacksmith's Yard, a cul-de-sac-courtyard survivor from 18th-century Derby. The yard was refashioned and updated in the 1980s, but still manages to look a little Dickensian.

The distinctive half-timbered house in the yard is home to BPM Records, a long-established second-hand vinyl and CD shop that buys and sells anything from jazz, ska, blues, funk and soul through to rock, punk and reggae – but not classical; there's a separate singles section too. The shop spreads over two floors and everything is clearly labelled and sorted thanks to the efforts of the owner, Dave Hill, who is friendly, well informed and helpful. Reward your craving for vinyl whenever you can.

Address BPM Records, 10 Old Blacksmith's Yard, Derby, DE1 3PD, +44 (0)1332 987229, www.bpmderby.com | Getting there A 10-minute walk from Derby bus station | Hours Mon–Fri 10am–4pm, Sat 10am–5pm | Tip Locals rarely if ever notice, but 'gate' – as in Sadler Gate – is a reference to the Danish settlement of the East Midlands: in Danish 'gata' means street. Ponder these historical niceties at the Standing Order pub at 28 Iron Gate.

# 89 Shardlow Heritage Centre

*Down by the riverside*

Very different from its immediate neighbours, the village of Shardlow, seven miles southeast of Derby, nudges up to the River Trent at a point from where the river is navigable all the way down to the Humber estuary. This geographical bonanza ensured there was river traffic hereabouts from time immemorial and, indeed, a magnificent Bronze Age log boat was discovered among the gravel pits just south of the village in 1998.

River traffic was one thing, but what transformed Shardlow's fortunes was the opening of the Trent and Mersey Canal in 1777. Around 93 miles long, this canal – the T&M – sliced across northwest England to link the rivers Mersey and Trent via Derwent Mouth near Shardlow (or 'Rural Rotterdam' as it was sometimes referred to). An ambitious venture, the T&M required 70 locks and 5 tunnels and stirred a real buzz of interest among the leading industrialists of the day – the famous canal engineer James Brindley designed it and no less a figure than Josiah Wedgwood cut the first sod.

For 70 years or so, until the railways forced the canals into decline, Shardlow boomed as an inland port for the trans-shipment of goods between the canal and the river. Those heady days are recalled at the Shardlow Heritage Centre, in the earliest of the surviving canal warehouses at the centre of the village. Thereafter, you can explore Shardlow on foot – either as the fancy takes you or by following the four-mile-long village trail as outlined on Heritage Centre leaflets.

There are around 50 Grade II-listed structures in Shardlow, including bridges and pubs, cottages and warehouses, a few Georgian mansions and the large and distinctive Clock Warehouse, once a warehouse then a corn mill. There are easy and charming canal towpath walks in either direction also, with one scenic choice being the 40-minute stroll east from the Clock Tower to Derwent Mouth.

**Address** Shardlow Heritage Centre, London Road, Shardlow, Derby, DE72 2GA, www.shardlowheritage.eclipse.co.uk | **Getting there** Shardlow is about 7 miles southeast of Derby on the A50 | **Hours** Footpaths – open access; Heritage Centre Easter–end Oct Sat, Sun & Bank Holidays noon–5pm | **Tip** Shardlow prides itself on its antique pubs, with the amenable New Inn, by the canal at 61 The Wharf (www.thenewinnshardlowpub.co.uk), offering an excellent range of beers. Some people say the food at the neighbouring Malt Shovel, 49 The Wharf, is better than that of the New Inn.

# 90 Smiths of Derby

*Clockmaking excellence*

Derby born and bred, John Smith (1813–1886) cut his horological spurs as an apprentice to the Whitehursts, an influential local family who ran a much-admired clock and watchmaking company. The young John Smith learnt well and saved hard until, in the 1850s, he was in a position to establish his own business at 37 Queen Street; the Whitehursts moved out of watchmaking shortly afterwards. In the event, John was to lay the foundations of a clock and watch-making company that would last for generations – and still flourishes today. His particular skill was in the matter of tower clocks in which his designs had a better power-to-weight ratio than any of his rivals' – clockmaking has always been a highly complex affair. John's mechanical skills were a recipe for commercial success and his two sons, Frank (1852–1913) and John (1857–1910), were similarly adept, their main clockmaking claim to fame being the huge – and very reliable – turret clock at St Paul's Cathedral.

Next up in the firm came Howard Smith (1907–1983), who developed an auto-wind system for clock towers, thereby eliminating the need for regular visits to wind them up – a major cost saving if ever there was one. Howard was also involved in the creation of a new clock and carillon for Derby's All Saints' church when it became a cathedral in 1927. Howard's two blue and gold clock faces still stare out over the city from the cathedral tower today; with surpassing skill, each is painted directly onto the stone by Smith of Derby employees.

These clock faces represent the traditional side of the company, but venture out to the Royal Derby Hospital, on Uttoxeter Road, and you can't but help but notice Smith's soaring, 22-foot high, LED, tulip-like contemporary pedestal clock positioned beside the hospital entrance; it's a bold venture – all credit to this dynamic, enterprising company.

**Address** Smith of Derby maintains several prestige clocks in its home town. The most notable are the Cathedral tower clock, 18–19 Iron Gate, Derby, DE1 3GP; and the pedestal clock at the main entrance to the Royal Derby Hospital, Uttoxeter Road, Derby, DE22 3NE. | **Getting there** The Cathedral is in the city centre, a few minutes' walk from Derby bus station; the Royal Derby Hospital is 3 miles to the south west of the city centre | **Hours** Both clocks are always accessible | **Tip** It's a surprise to see that one of the neighbourhoods near the Royal Derby Hospital is called 'California' and has been since the 1880s. No one is entirely sure how this came about, but it may have something to do with a handful of Derby men charging off to join the California Gold Rush in the 1840s.

# 91 South Wingfield

*One village; one manor house; one railway station*

The hamlet of South Wingfield, around 16 miles north of Derby, has a country air, its medley of old cottages and stone boundary walls hinting at its long rural history, rather than more recent times when the local pit – Wingfield Manor Colliery (1906–1963) – was the biggest employer. Long before king coal, there was Wingfield Manor House, now dramatic ruins, but once the opulent residence of the earls of Shrewsbury. It was the sixth earl who made the biggest historical splash when he was obliged to hold Mary, Queen of Scots, under what amounted to house arrest for no less than 15 years. The ruins of his house, which date from the 15th century and include a 69-foot tower, are a delight to explore, or at least they would be if they were open. English Heritage has decided that the ruins are too dangerous and have closed them until further notice – check their website for the latest.

The Manor House may be temporarily closed, but there's compensation on the other side of the village in the form of Wingfield Station, one of the earliest surviving railway stations in the world, built for the North Midland Railway in the 1830s. The station pre-dates the rage for the neo-Gothic with Francis Thompson (1808–1895), the architect, opting for an elegant classical style and an interior that feels very villa-like and domestic. The talented Thompson specialised in all things railway, building 13 stations for the North Midland Railway, of which this is the only one to have survived.

The station was closed in 1967 and fell into disrepair until a spirited campaign led by the Derbyshire Historic Buildings Trust (DHBT) saved the building, which has now been restored and turned into a tea room and small shop – and very good home-made scones they serve too. The only surprise is that trains still go through the station at regular intervals.

**Address** Wingfield Station, off Holme Lane, South Wingfield, DE55 7NY, +44 (0)7592 658778, www.derbyshirehistoricbuildingstrust.org.uk/wingfield-station-project; Wingfield Manor House, off Garner Lane, South Wingfield DE55 7NH, www.english-heritage.org.uk | **Getting there** Wingfield Station is clearly signed down a short lane off Holme Lane (B5035) on the east side of the village; Wingfield Manor is signposted off Garner Lane (B5035) on the south side of the village | **Hours** Wingfield Station open Wed–Sun 10am–4.30pm; Wingfield Manor currently viewable only from a distance – it is part of a working farm, so please respect the owners' privacy | **Tip** Look out for the large, stone monument in the car park of Wingfield Station. It's the grandiloquent crest of the North Midland Railway that was somehow retrieved from Derby station when it was rebuilt in 1892.

# 92 St Alkmund's Well

*Holy waters*

Quite why one Anglo-Saxon king should be beatified and not another can be something of a mystery, but Northumbria's St Alkmund (c. 774–800) seems to have made a cracking start in the saintly race by being a thoroughly good egg: legend has him giving to the poor, protecting orphans and ruling with humility. Alkmund also improved his saintly odds by wanting to be a Christian martyr, managing to get himself killed on the battlefield after his peace-making efforts between rival princes failed. Naturally, and in the way of such things, the spot where Alkmund died was the scene of multiple miracles, and when Alkmund was reinterred, guess what – a beautiful fragrance issued from his tomb.

Nevertheless, St Alkmund might still have been forgotten had it not been for the efforts of Aethelfleda (870–918), both the daughter of Alfred the Great and the ruler of Mercia. Her lands were mightily troubled by marauding Danes and it seems likely that she wanted to champion an Anglo-Saxon saint to raise morale. Whatever the case, St Alkmund's earthly remains went on a dizzying spin, being transported here and there before ending up in Derby at St Alkmund's Church, on Bridgegate. The saint's shrine did not survive the Reformation and the church was itself demolished in 1846, but not before the vicar, the long-serving (and irascible) Henry Cantrell (1684–1762), kept the saint's memory alive by repairing the ancient well – St Alkmund's Well – which was near to his church.

Today, sight of St Alkmund's Well is unlikely to set your pulse racing, but it is an interesting moment: surrounded by railings, the well with its trickle of water lies just three steps down below street level with trees on the side. Legend asserts that this is the precise spot where the body of St Alkmund was rested by the bearers when it arrived on the edge of Derby, but no one knows for sure.

**Address** Bath Street, at its junction with Well Street, Derby, DE1 3FG | **Getting there** A 15-minute walk north of Derby Market Place via Sowter Road | **Hours** Always accessible | **Tip** There's a Well Dressing ceremony at St Alkmund's Well once a year – in late May. Details from Visit Derby (www.visitderby.co.uk). The 'dressing' of wells and springs with pictures made from natural materials like petals and leaves is a traditional Derbyshire custom.

# 93_St Bartholomew, Elvaston

*Derbyshire feuding*

Dating from the 13th century, the pocket-sized parish church of St Bartholomew sits tight against Elvaston Castle amid its Country Park. From the outside, it's the church's splendid Gothic tower that catches the eye, but within it's the reredos (screen), an ornate whopper by that champion of the Gothic Revival, George Frederick Bodley (1827–1907), who worked on St Bartholomew's in 1904–05.

It was the Stanhope family who ruled the Elvaston roost for centuries, living here until 1939, so it's no surprise that most of the church's memorials honour one member of the clan or another, the lengths of their epitaphs not necessarily reflecting their importance or ability. Neither did all of them stick to the 'Stanhope' name – some family heads were the earls of Chesterfield, others – like the present one – the Earl of Harrington.

In the church, look out for the tomb of John Stanhope (1590–1638), whose partly armoured, alabaster figure looks clumsy and out of kilter. This misalignment dates back to the Civil War, when Parliamentary soldiers vandalised Stanhope's tomb during a raid on Royalist Elvaston and the subsequent repairs were cack handed. The raid was organised by the Parliamentary commander John Gell out of personal malice rather than military strategy – the Civil War may have been ideological elsewhere, but not in Derbyshire, where one set of landed gentry slugged it out with another.

A further highlight is the immaculately carved wall monument dedicated to Charles Stanhope, an army officer and the 3rd Earl of Harrington (1753–1829). It depicts a grieving Athena, the Goddess of War, with a Medusa on the boss of her shield. This is the work of Rome's Antonio Canova (1757–1822), the most famous neo-classical sculptor of his day. There are only a handful of Canovas in England, and when and how this one got here is not entirely clear.

**Address** St Bartholomew's Church, Borrowash Road, Elvaston, Derby, DE72 3EP, +44 (0)1332 792658, www.trentderwentparishes.org | **Getting there** Elvaston Castle and Country Park is 8 miles from Derby – there's parking inside the park near the castle and the castle is yards from the church | **Hours** For opening times and guided tours check the website | **Tip** Sir John Gell, the leader of Derbyshire's Parliamentary forces, was widely disliked by both sides, especially after he had the body of a Royalist commander paraded through Derby. The Gells' family home was Hopton Hall, a rambling mansion in the centre of Derbyshire that is open to visitors (www.hoptonhall.co.uk).

# 94_St Helen's House

*Georgian architecture at its most charming*

St Helen's House is generally reckoned to be one of the most beautiful Georgian town houses in the Midlands, though admittedly it's now marooned beside a busy road on the north side of the city centre. The house is an imposing, stone-faced structure with a spectacular façade, whose graceful symmetries come complete with portico and pediments topped off with decorative parapet urns of cast iron. The house was completed in the Palladian style in 1767 to a design by the architect Joseph Pickford (1734–1782), who spent years working on the mansions of the rich here in Derbyshire. It was built for John Gisborne (1717–1779) – a local politician with aristocratic connections – but was soon passed to his son, the Reverend Thomas Gisborne (1758–1846).

Thomas Gisborne was a long-serving Anglican clergyman and leading member of the Clapham Sect, evangelical Christians who campaigned for social reform in general and the abolition of the slave trade in particular. The most influential member of the group was William Wilberforce and, partly as a result of the group's efforts, the slave trade was banned across the British Empire in 1807. Gisborne was also a polemicist of some repute, though his *An Enquiry into the Duties of the Female Sex*, stressing subordination, is hardly a go-to text today.

Later on, St Helen's House passed into the hands of another prominent local figure, the inventor and industrialist William Strutt (1756–1830). Strutt proceeded to enlarge the house considerably and there were yet more modifications after Derby Grammar School bought the place in 1863 – hence the matching buildings that stand close by. The school stayed here for just over a century, leaving behind a modest war memorial to those old boys who had died; it's located in front of the main house, which now holds offices. The blue plaque remembers both Thomas Gisborne and William Strutt.

**Address** King Street, Derby, DE1 3EE | **Getting there** A 15-minute walk from Derby bus station | **Hours** Exterior always viewable but no public access | **Tip** From St Helen's House, it's the briefest of strolls to St Mary's Catholic Church, Bridge Gate (www.stmarysparish.co.uk), whose soaring tower – in the Perpendicular Gothic style – was the work of none other than Augustus Pugin; pop inside to view the handsome five-bay nave.

# 95 St Mary on the Bridge

*A rare survivor*

In medieval England, it was far from unusual for a church to be built on a bridge, but only half a dozen survive – and one of them is Derby's Chapel of St Mary on the Bridge, near the city centre on the west bank of the River Derwent. There seems to have been a chapel here from at least the 13th century, but its heyday was two centuries later when the chapel became a noted place of pilgrimage, home to both an anchorite cell and a revered icon, the Black Virgin of Derby.

The Reformation swept icon and cell away, but just in case local Catholics missed the religious point, three recusant Catholic priests – Nicholas Garlick, Robert Ludlam and Richard Simpson – were hanged, drawn and quartered outside the chapel in 1588. Curiously, two of the priests were arrested in north Derbyshire by George Talbot, the Earl of Shrewsbury and the fourth husband of the redoubtable Bess of Hardwick. The priestly trio, the 'Padley Martyrs', were beatified by the pope in 1987.

From the early 17th century onwards, the chapel became increasingly neglected, odd-jobbing as lodgings, a workshop and a storeroom until a thoroughgoing restoration of 1929–30 produced some degree of order in the tangled mix of rough stonework and red brick you see today; the large and good-looking T-shaped former clergy house next door was upgraded at the same time. The chapel's dinky little wooden door is the exterior's most charming feature, though the best view is actually on the far side of the river, from where the chapel's attractive half-timbered gable end comes into proper view. The interior of St Mary on the Bridge is narrow and angular, the highlight being the stained glass of the east window, whose brightly coloured, semi-abstract design was the work of Mary Dobson (1912–1977), an English painter and illustrator who came to specialise in stained glass and mosaics.

Address Duke Street, Derby, DE1 3AT, www.derbycathedral.org/discover/the-bridge-chapel | Getting there A 5-minute walk from the Cathedral | Hours Hours vary – see website for times – but normally Sat 10.30am–2.30pm | Tip While you are visiting the chapel, be sure to have a good look at St Mary's bridge, a handsome stone structure whose three sweeping arches date back to the 1780s.

# 96_St Mary's Gate

*Dignified Derby*

Running west from the Cathedral, St Mary's Gate has a sort of sombre dignity that's markedly different from the rest of the city centre, its sequence of old and handsome red-brick buildings reflecting its past importance for all things civic and legal. On the north side of the street, the first building of interest is St Mary's Chambers, where a legal practice is lodged within an attractive early 19th-century villa of crumbling brick with stone-trimmed windows. There's a matching terrace on the other side of the street too, but here there are also Georgian flourishes in the fancy columns of a stone portico and a double doorway.

Further along the street, the Cathedral Quarter Hotel occupies a grand red-brick and stone-edged structure in the style of a country mansion and complete with an elaborate portico and a roof-top balustrade. Pleasing to the eye, it was built in the 1890s as council offices – with additional offices located in the rather more subdued building opposite.

Nearby stands one of Derby's finest buildings, the former Shire Hall, whose delightful five-bay stone façade with its finely carved twin doorways is seen to fine advantage from across its front courtyard. Since its construction as an assize court in the 1650s, in the last years of Cromwell's Protectorate, the Shire Hall has been much modified and used for a variety of purposes – it is now the Southern Derbyshire Magistrates' Court – but bits and pieces of the old have survived in good condition. One is the monument to Francis Noel Clarke Mundy (1739–1815), a long-serving magistrate, whose epitaph trumpets the (notional) values of the Enlightenment: 'This excellent Man admired for the elegance of his literary Productions, beloved for the gentleness of his Manners, revered for his public and private Virtues lived happily… to the age of 76 years. May his Example excite Emulation.'

**Address** St Mary's Gate, Derby, DE1 3JR | **Getting there** A 10-minute walk from Derby bus station | **Hours** Always accessible; limited public access to the public galleries at the Southern Derbyshire Magistrates' Court, The Court House, St Mary's Gate, (Mon–Fri 9am–5pm) | **Tip** In *Adam Bede*, the novelist George Eliot (1819–1880) had Hetty Sorrel tried for child murder in the Shire Hall on St Mary's Gate. Eliot was born in Nuneaton, 40 miles from Derby.

# 97 St Matthew's, Morley

*Oh! The exquisite stained glass*

The rambling hamlet of Morley, just five miles from Derby, sits amid the uplands separating the former textile towns of the Trent Valley from the coalfields to the north. There were small stone quarries near the village from early days, but mostly it was farming, presided over by the local lords – the Morleys and ultimately the Sacheverells. One of the latter, John Sacheverell, was killed at the Battle of Bosworth Field in 1485, but this didn't create as much of a fuss as the subsequent abduction of his wife, Jane, and her enforced marriage to a certain William Willoughby of Wollaton, in Nottingham. King Henry VII took exception to these goings-on, not so much because of Jane, but more because Willoughby took control of her property from the moment he married her.

The main reason to visit Morley today is the church of St Matthew, whose sturdy spire rises high into the sky at the end of a narrow lane. The church is a mix of architectural styles from the Normans onwards, but its real glory is the stained glass windows of the north aisle. Here, one window tells the tale of the Invention of the Holy Cross and another relates the story of the hermit-saint Robert of Knaresborough with its deer and hunting, gamekeepers and king. In the vestry, there's more stained glass, in this case honouring St John of Bridlington, a 14th-century priest and general miracle worker.

The stained glass was commissioned for a nearby abbey until, at the Dissolution, the Sacheverells bought the windows and moved them here lock, stock and barrel. The windows possess the startling immediacy typical of medieval art – and so do many of the church's brasses, most notably that of a kneeling John Stathum and his wife in the north chapel. Also in this chapel are several exquisite, finely carved tomb chests, including one for Jacynth Sacheverell (d.1656), shown recumbent with his wife, his kneeling children down below.

Address St Matthew's Church, Church Lane, Morley, DE7 6DE, +44 (0)1332 889389, www.morley-church.co.uk | Getting there St Matthew's Church is a 5-mile drive northeast of Derby | Hours Church opening hours vary – consult the website | Tip The sturdy, Gothic Revival sandstone structure in front of the church is the Sacheverell-Bateman Mausoleum of 1897. This was built in memory of Hugh Alleyne by his wife, Anna, following his death in a hunting accident when he was just 36.

# 98 St Michael's, Melbourne

*A handsome Norman church*

The exquisite church of St Michael with St Mary's is without doubt the star attraction in the small and well-heeled town of Melbourne, just nine miles south of Derby. The church stands spare and lean among a cluster of ancient dwellings and although there is some doubt as to when and by whom the church was built, it seems likely that the first version was finished in the mid-1130s on the orders of Henry I, one of England's Norman kings.

Inevitably, there have been some changes since then – parts of the chancel disappeared long ago and much of the roof was replaced in the 1630s – but St Michael's is in a remarkably fine state of preservation and Gilbert Scott's Victorian refurbishment, which took place between 1859 and 1862, was mercifully light fingered.

From the outside, St Michael's looks solid, almost sombre, but inside you are immediately struck by the beauty of the nave, whose strapping Norman columns – or piers – stride down to the central crossing with a flood of light bursting in from the clerestory windows up above. Between the piers, strong and heavy arches sport the dog-tooth decoration for which the Normans are famous, but here at Melbourne pride of place goes to the carvings on the capitals at the central crossing. Several of these have a scurrilous air, including the 'Melbourne cat', which may well have been an attempt to depict a lion, but then there's the remarkable sheela-na-gig, in which a grimacing woman is depicted legs akimbo, vulva prominent and vine leaves protruding from her mouth. There are only 50-odd sheela-na-gigs in the whole of England and no one is entirely certain as to their meaning. Some experts think they were to ward off death, evil and demons, others that they hark back to pre-Christian thought and rituals, with a combination of the two being equally likely. They were particularly popular in Anglo-Norman churches like this one.

Address St Michael with St Mary, Church Square, Melbourne, DE73 8JH, +44 (0)1332 862153, www.melbourneparishchurch.org.uk | Getting there Melbourne is a 9-mile drive from Derby | Hours Normally open Mon–Fri 9am–5pm, Sat 9am–3.30 or 4pm (advisable to check the website) | Tip The church walls were once covered in murals and although most are lost, one has been retrieved and it's at the central crossing. A strange affair, it shows two women arguing over a stolen Host (the wafer used in the Mass), while a horned devil readies himself to punish them.

# 99_Staunton Harold Estate

*Bitterness in the countryside*

On a sunny day, it would be hard to imagine a more tranquil scene than the easy rolling countryside of Staunton Harold Estate, on the Derbyshire/Leicestershire border, about 16 miles south of Derby. It's true that the landscape may not be all that it seems – there's artifice in the planting of the trees and in the shape of Fish Pond lake – but it's a delightful spot all the same. The estate is popular with walkers, many of whom stroll across the lake by means of the sweetest of narrow footbridges, before popping into the garden centre and browsing the old stables, now the Ferrers Centre for Arts and Crafts.

Staunton Harold Hall dominates proceedings, a large and imposing 18th-century country house that looks much better than it has any right to, considering its bumpy history. For centuries, the Hall was owned by the Shirley family, the Earls Ferrers, but they were a wayward bunch: one of them disappeared to modernise the Persian army and another was a privateer who came to a sticky end. Yet, for sheer cussedness it was Sir Robert Shirley (1623–1656) who takes the biscuit. An ardent Royalist, Shirley simply could not abide the result of the Civil War – and he did something about it: he built a church opposite his house with a sturdy, battlemented tower and a wood-panelled interior, all in the Gothic style, and then above the west doorway he attached a plaque declaring his hatred of the Protectorate: 'In the yeare 1653 when all things sacred were throughout ye nation Either demollisht or profaned, Sir Robert Shirley Baronet founded this church whose singular praise it is to have done the best thing in ye worst times.'

Such flagrant hatred of Cromwell was never going to endear him to the authorities, who had Shirley imprisoned on six occasions; he died in the Tower of London, though Charles II restored the family fortunes at the Restoration.

Address Staunton Harold Estate, Calke Road, Melbourne, DE73 8DL, www.stauntonharoldestate.co.uk | Getting there Staunton Harold is a 16-mile drive south from Derby | Hours Estate opening hours normally 8am–5pm, but check website; church usually Apr–Oct Sun noon–3pm (www.nationaltrust.org.uk) | Tip For refreshments, there is a café on the estate inside the Ferrers Centre for Arts and Crafts (www.ferrerscentre.co.uk). There is also a garden centre, picture framers and deli here.

# 100_The Strand

*A slice of Victorian Derby*

Short and sweet, The Strand is one of Derby's most appealing streets, running south to north across a segment of the city centre. It starts where it meets Wardwick with the Refuge Assurance building, a sterling, three-storey stone affair that skilfully curves round the junction, its roof crested with ornamental ironwork. Finished in 1878, and with a design based on that of Burlington Arcade in London, the Refuge was created by Giles and Brookhouse, a local firm that specialised in Gothic Revival churches, so this very secular commission, which created the Italianate structure you see today, may well have been a welcome change of architectural diet. It was well paid too: insurance and assurance companies had just pioneered the sale of inexpensive policies to the working classes, a lucrative business that prompted the most important of them, including the Refuge, to establish prestige offices in any number of towns and cities.

Proceeding north west, two matching stone terraces of dignified Italianate design frame The Strand until one side fizzles out, though the other – on the east side of the street – keeps going, performing a gentle curve that incorporates the really rather grand stone entrance to The Strand Arcade.

Completed in 1878, the arcade comprises a short and sheltered passageway that runs down to Sadler Gate lined by attractive shop fronts, all set beneath a glass roof. It was a commercial venture funded by one of Derby's most prominent Victorians, the redoubtable Sir Abraham Woodiwiss (1828–1884). The epitome of the self-made man, Woodiwiss started out as a stonemason, but went on to make a fortune as a railway contractor – it was his company that built the famous Settle to Carlisle line. Sir Abraham was mayor from 1880–1882, but his last years were far from comfortable on account of the gout that contributed to his early demise.

**Address** The Strand, Derby, DE1 1BE | **Getting there** A 10-minute walk from Derby bus station | **Hours** Always accessible | **Tip** The Woodiwiss family also got into house building, and the attractive terraced villas of Hartington Street, on the south side of the city, are the best surviving example of their work.

# 101 Swarkestone Bridge

*A long bridge – but not too far*

Swarkestone Bridge spans the marshy flood plain of the River Trent about six miles south of Derby and is, as Pevsner described it, 'a remarkable example of medieval public works'.

The bridge over the Trent and the adjoining causeway is three-quarters of a mile long, making it the longest medieval bridge in England. Its various swerves are guarded by low-lying stone battlements and cutwaters. The causeway dates back to the early 13th century with the first version probably made of wood. A stone version arrived a few decades later, since when it has been modified and repaired on numerous occasions. The causeway was strategically important, so repairs were funded by the levelling of tolls under royal decree, but several of the 17 supporting sandstone arches are original – or at least medieval. The bridge, on the other hand, was entirely rebuilt in the neo-classical style after flood damage in the 1790s; the architect was the bridge specialist Thomas Harrison (1744–1829), who had been greatly influenced by his studies in Rome.

Swarkestone Bridge also witnessed a battle, when the Royalists failed to hold it against the Parliamentarians, and a famous retreat – Bonnie Prince Charlie's Highlanders rushed the bridge but never went further south.

Rather more diverting is the legend regarding the bridge's origins. This has two women, the Bellamont sisters, engaged to be married. They decide to throw a joint celebration, but their fiancés are, in the way of such things, on the other side of the River Trent. Needless to say, the men's attempt to ford the river on horseback ends in disaster with both being swept away and drowned. Grief stricken, the sisters are determined that no one else should suffer in this way again, so they build a bridge – but this is not a Disney tale: the sisters don't find love, the bridge bankrupts them and they die penniless.

Address Swarkestone Bridge, Derby, DE73 7HX | Getting there It's a 10-mile drive from Derby to Swarkestone Bridge | Hours Always accessible | Tip Swarkestone Bridge used to be on the main road between Derby and Coventry. This is no longer the case, but it still gets mighty busy. The best vantage point is near the north end of the bridge – keep your eyes peeled.

# 102 Swarkestone Church

*Intricate alabaster tombs*

The light scattering of dwellings that make up Swarkestone village string out along the north side of the River Trent to either side of Swarkestone Bridge. A quiet corner of Derbyshire today, there's little indication that this was once a main route across the Midlands from Derby to Coventry. Neither does the village church of St James command much initial attention: tucked away down a narrow country lane, it's an attractive enough structure with a strong, crenellated medieval tower, but the outside of the nave looks drab following a heavy-handed, 19th-century refit. But don't give up. The immaculately maintained interior, with its half-timbered ceiling, stained glass and pointed arches is charming and owes much to the care and attention the Victorians lavished upon it.

Even better, St James holds several wonderful and wonderfully well-preserved alabaster tomb-chests. The stone for these came from neighbouring Chellaston, now a suburb of Derby but once one of the country's largest sources of quarried alabaster, a soft stone popular with local sculptors for being easy to work. Among the tomb-chests is a fascinating memorial to John of Rolleston (d. 1482), who is shown in his armour recumbent next to Susan, his wife. Both figures are beautifully incised in black against the off-white of the alabaster. Nearby is the tomb of Sir John Harpur (1546–c.1622), one of the more important members of the family, who had one or two hairy moments in his avowal of evangelical Protestantism during the reign of James I.

The tomb of Sir John and his wife Isabel is the most finely carved of the lot with the knight squeezed into his armour below an intricate ruff and up to the carved hairs on his head. On the chest below Sir John are his 12 children – 7 sons and 5 daughters – tiny and exquisite statuettes flecked with ancient colour.

Address St James' Church, Church Lane, Swarkestone, DE73 7GT, +44 (0)1332 792658, www.trentderwentparishes.org | Getting there St James' Church is down Church Lane, off the Swarkestone Road (A514), a 9-mile drive south of Derby; bus 2 or 70 from Derby bus station to the Cottage Garage and a 5-minute walk | Hours Limited opening hours (see www.trentderwentparishes.org) | Tip St James' Church is just 5 miles from Donington Park Motorpoint Circuit, Castle Donington, where they have a varied programme of motorsport races and rock festivals (www.donington-park.co.uk).

# 103 Swarkestone Pavilion

*Anyone for bowls?*

A real architectural surprise, the enchanting Swarkestone Pavilion, visible from an A-road about nine miles south of Derby, sits at the head of a walled rectangular enclosure within a large and grassy field. The Pavilion – also known as the Stand or the Grandstand – was built between 1630 and 1632 for the local bigwig, Sir John Harpur, whose country house, of which only the battered ruins survive, was 200 yards or so to the rear. An exercise in delicate symmetries, the Pavilion is built from local gritstone with sandstone facings at the front. Very much in the Jacobean manner, its most fetching feature is its shapely pair of towers with their dinky, lead-green cupolas, though the columned loggia and the cross windows come a close second.

There has been much debate as to quite what the pavilion was built for and to what subsequent purposes it has been put. It may well have been built to celebrate John Harpur's marriage as a combined banqueting house and grandstand from where games of bowls could be observed on the adjacent walled bowling green – known as The Cuttle. Later, the Pavilion may have become part of a formal garden, though the supporting evidence here is scant, and there have also been suggestions that it was the grandstand for several gory sports – bull-baiting, bear-baiting and deer coursing.

The Pavilion suffered from the vicissitudes of the Harpur family, who abandoned their Swarkestone house in the 1710s, preferring their Calke estates instead. In 1844, it was struck by lightning and subsequently fell into dereliction, no matter that the Rolling Stones staged a photo shoot here in preparation for the release of their *Beggar's Banquet* album in 1968. Redemption came in the form of the Landmark Trust, who acquired and then refurbished the Pavilion in 1985; the trust now rents the building out as holiday accommodation.

Address Swarkestone, Derby, DE73 7JB | Getting there Swarkestone Pavilion is a 9-mile drive south of Derby | Hours Exterior always accessible; rentable through the Landmark Trust (www.landmarktrust.org.uk) | Tip From the Pavilion, it's a 10-minute walk along a narrow country lane to the prettiness of the Trent & Mersey Canal and the Swarkestone Locks.

# 104 Ticknall

*A quaint and fascinating village*

Tiny Ticknall, about 13 miles from Derby, sits amid rolling countryside, its long and slender High Street flanked by an assortment of old and pretty cottages. For most of its history, Ticknall has been an estate village owned by the Harpur Crewes of neighbouring Calke Abbey. In the way of such things, sometimes the Harpur Crewe in charge was fair and generous, sometimes not, but you can bet the villagers had a good old gossip about Sir Vauncey Harpur Crewe, the 10th Baronet (1846–1924). Eccentric and often disagreeable, this particular Harpur Crewe threw one of his daughters out of Calke Abbey for smoking a cigarette and blew a fortune on a natural history collection, stumping up the enormous sum of 300 guineas for the egg of a great auk in 1894.

In 1985, the family ceded Calke Abbey to the National Trust in settlement of death duties and since then the character of the village has slowly changed, though its standout curiosity remains Main Street's 'Lock-Up'. Built in 1809, this dinky octagonal brick structure, with its pantomime roof, was where local miscreants were imprisoned overnight. At some point, there was a change of heart, so it was turned into storage space for road sweeping tools – apart, that is, from the time when the Home Guard stored their weapons here during World War II.

Ticknall may be countrified today, but in the 18th century it was something of an industrial centre with brick yards and lime quarries. This spawned the Ticknall Tramway, an early version of a railway in which goods were moved the 13 miles to the Ashby canal by horse on a narrow-gauge tramway with cast-iron rails. Operating from 1802 to 1913, bits and pieces of the tramway have survived – including some tunnelling under Calke Park – but the most conspicuous reminder is the Ticknall Arc, the sandstone and brick arch that loops over Main Street (A514).

**Address** The Lock-Up, Main Street, just east of Church Lane, Ticknall, DE73 7JU | **Getting there** Ticknall is 10 miles from Derby via the A514 | **Hours** Always accessible | **Tip** Ticknall also had a thriving pottery industry in the 18th century and a representative sample of this Ticknall Ware can be seen 5 miles from the village at Sharpe's Pottery Heritage and Arts Trust, 23 West Street, Swadlincote, DE11 9DG (www.sharpespotterymuseum.org.uk).

# 105 Toyota at Burnaston

*David Bookbinder brings Toyota to Derby*

Drive south west from Derby on the A38 and you'll soon leave the city's suburbs behind for the easy countryside of south Derbyshire. Here, hidden from view just off the road at tiny Burnaston, is the main UK factory of the Japanese car giant Toyota. Opened in late 1992, the plant has produced more than five million vehicles over its lifetime and currently employs around 2,500 people in what has proved to be a major boost to the local economy. The negotiations that brought Toyota here were long winded and convoluted. There were sweeteners for the deal – a slab of easy-to-develop land near Derby for starters, not to mention access to a skilled local workforce – but it would almost certainly never have happened had it not been for the negotiating skills of David Bookbinder (1941–2023).

A conviction politician, Bookbinder did not have to consult focus groups to decide what he believed and what he wanted to do, his left-wing radicalism deeply felt and acted upon. He was elected to Derbyshire County Council as a Labour Party Councillor in 1973 and became the leader in 1981; he stayed in power for 11 years. Landing Toyota is usually considered his greatest success, but there were many others, not least an inspirational reorganisation of the Youth Service – of which this author had some personal experience – and his dogged support of the striking miners during the Miners' Strike of 1984.

Inevitably, Bookbinder had many enemies, and the right-wing press repeatedly maligned and slandered him, though, as some compensation, he did win significant damages from the *Sunday Times*, who had accused him of corruption. For the man himself, his greatest achievement was the banning of corporal punishment in Derbyshire schools; as Bookbinder said: 'Think about it. It was common practice in this country to educate children by beating them. How sick can you get?'

Address Vehicle Plant, Toyota Motor Manufacturing, Burnaston, DE1 9TA, +44 (0)1332 282121, www.toyotauk.com | Getting there The Toyota Vehicle Plant is a 20-minute drive southwest of Derby | Hours Viewable from the outside only; occasional tours (check the website) | Tip From Burnaston, it's a 10-minute drive to the spankingly new Mercia Marina (www.merciamarina.co.uk), a leisure complex, where a shoal of narrowboats gather on Willington Lake, off Findern Lane, DE65 6DW.

# 106_Vernon Gate

*Lock 'em up*

If you've been weaned on Jane Austen's period dramas, then the brutal force of Georgian Derby's Vernon Gate, on Vernon Street, might come as a surprise. After the shock of the French Revolution, the town's middle class felt uneasy and insecure. They took one look at the Friar Gate prison and realised it just wouldn't do – it was far too cramped and chaotic – so they set about building the fortress-like Vernon Street County Gaol instead. Work began in 1823 and took four years under the direction of Francis Goodwin (1784–1835), one of the most competitive architects of his day: Goodwin was well known for chasing commissions and undercutting his rivals, all with a rare ferocity that may have contributed to the apoplexy that finally finished him off.

Goodwin's prison was big and bold, but only the front has survived, a heavy-duty, single-storey stone structure whose broad geometric shapes and massive gateway reveal French neo-classical influences. It's hard to imagine anything more formidable looking, though the round towers at either end of the façade were actually added in the aftermath of the Reform Riots of 1831, when the rioters had gathered threateningly outside the prison gates.

The Vernon Street prison closed in 1919 and was all but demolished nine years later. In its time, the prison handled a fair old bagatelle of capital offences, from forgery and bestiality through to murder, horse stealing, highway robbery, theft and rape. The prison also picked up a number of 'lasts': the last public execution in Derby took place here in 1862 and the last person to be hanged here was William Slack in 1907. You have also got to feel especially sorry for a certain Thomas Hulley, who was transported to Australia; he managed to escape back to England, a considerable achievement in its own right, but he was then betrayed and promptly hanged.

**Address** Vernon Gate, Vernon Street, Derby, DE1 1UQ | **Getting there** A 20-minute walk from Derby bus station | **Hours** Always accessible | **Tip** Vernon Street, the approach to Vernon Gate, is wide and really rather elegant, framed on both sides by Regency-style houses.

# 107 The War Memorial

*The dear and long departed*

The wide-open spaces of Derby's Market Place seem irresistible to street furniture of one sort or another, but the one real stand-out is the splendid War Memorial, stuck on a pedestal directly in front of the Guildhall. A poignant statue with more than a hint of Art Deco, the memorial was unveiled in 1924 shortly after the end of World War I, when every city and town in the UK was mourning its grievous losses.

The memorial incorporates a bronze sculpture by London's George Arthur Walker (1861–1939) of what has usually been described as a Virgin and Child, but in fact, this Virgin and Child were probably meant to represent a typical English mother and child, which would at least explain the woman's unusual head gear. Curiously, Walker became something of a war memorial specialist, churning out a fair number of them, mostly across the Midlands. The figures are themselves attached to a plain, stone Celtic cross, which adds a sombre tone – all to an overall design by a local architect, one Charles Clayton Thompson (1873–1932).

Huge crowds congregated here when the War Memorial was unveiled, fulfilling the Market Place's traditional function as the city's main gathering point. During its long history, the Market Place has seen pretty much everything, from riots and executions through to protests and public meetings, but nothing perhaps as bizarre as the Shrovetide Football Match, which used to kick off here every year and involved thousands of locals divided into two teams – the north enders and the south enders. The game went on for two days; the goals were a mile apart; and the troublesome drank and fought, fought and drank, with others throwing soot, flour or coloured dyes at the team they opposed. Yet the match always made the magistrates fidgety, so finally, in 1846, they brought in the army and suppressed the game once and for all.

Address Market Place, Derby, DE1 3AS | Getting there A 5-minute walk from Derby bus station | Hours Always accessible | Tip Derby's Shrovetide Football Match may have been suppressed, but it continues in Ashbourne, a small town 14 miles north west of Derby – and a boisterous business it is too.

# 108 The Wardwick

*Victorian confidence; Jacobean elegance*

Standing tall and grand on the Wardwick is one of Derby's most self-confident Victorian structures, an imposing and surprisingly ornate edifice built in the 1870s as Derby's Central Library, a function it served until 2018. From the outside, the dominant feature is the splendid Flemish–Gothic central tower, a whopping affair topped by a set of pirouetting mini-roofs. Down below, the bulk of the façade is of softly-hued, orange-red brick, but this is spiced up by stone dressings, terracotta tile panels and an arched entrance set beneath a bulging oriel window. Beyond the entrance, the capacious interior is given a sense of drama by the mezzanine balcony, where light cascades down from the glass roof above.

The architect responsible was a certain young Londoner Richard Knill Freeman (1840–1904), who had enjoyed a very modest career until he landed this prestigious contract: the influence of the Duke of Devonshire, who had just donated a mighty pile of books to the library, may have been crucial. Either way, Freeman's completed library was well received, sealing his reputation, while his liking for towers was appreciated by the Bolsheviks: in Moscow, his St Andrew's Anglican Church had a soaring tower, which the Bolsheviks climbed so that they could install a machine gun post at the start of the Russian Revolution.

Directly across the street from the old Central Library, at 35 Wardwick, is the Jacobean House, a handsome town house and Derby's first brick building dating back to the early 17th century. The house has endured several refurbishments, most recently to become student accommodation, but perhaps surprisingly, it is currently in good condition, its brickwork neat and trim, its stone dressings painted a bright white above a grand double doorway. For many years, this house was occupied by a branch of the prominent Gisborne family, social reformers par excellence.

Address Wardwick, Derby, DE1 1HS,www.derbymuseums.org/museum-and-art-gallery/venue-hire/the-wardwick | Getting there A 10-minute walk from Derby bus station | Hours Jacobean House & former Central Library viewable from the outside only, but the latter is available for hire, and hosts special events | Tip It's the briefest of strolls from the Wardwick to the sparkingly new Valliant Live, a 3,500-capacity entertainment venue on Colyear Street, DE1 1LA (https://vaillantlive.co.uk).

# 109 Winter's Photo Studio

*A fascinating photographic studio*

Something of a local institution, Winter's Photographic Studio is thought to be the longest running photography business in Britain.

It all began in 1852 when a Frenchman by the name of Emmanuel Nicolas Charles opened a photographic studio in what was then little more than a glorified shed. Charles did well and 10 years later he employed an assistant by the name of Walter William Winter (1824–1924). Suffolk-born, Winter took over the business in 1864 and moved into today's premises three years later. Several decades later, Winter sold up and moved to Canada, and the studio passed to the King family, who still own the business.

Much to the credit of the Kings, the studio has not been clumsily modernised, as witnessed by the exterior, where the vintage black and white painted façade incorporates a distinctive row of pointed windows. The interior has kept many of its old bits and pieces too, but the business is very much on the button, offering a wide variety of photographic services including portraits, passports and copying, restoration and picture framing; family portraiture is a particular speciality.

What makes Winter's remarkable is its extensive archive of old images, which reveal the changing face of Derbyshire from Victorian times onwards – anything and everything from studio portraits through to street scenes. There are some caches of particular interest – German prisoners of war interned in Derbyshire in World War I, for instance – but it's the sheer volume of early photos and glass plate negatives that has attracted so much attention. The studio was unable to provide for their proper care, storage and cataloguing, but in 2018 the Heritage Lottery Fund (HLF) stepped in with a significant grant to the newly formed W. W. Winter Heritage Trust. As the HLF explained: 'It is a hugely important historical collection.' Things now seem set fair.

Address 45 Midland Road, Derby, DE1 2SP, +44 (0)1332 345224, wwwinter.co.uk | Getting there A 5-minute walk from Derby railway station | Hours Tue–Fri 9am–3pm, Sat 9am–1pm and by appointment | Tip For further information about W. W. Winter's photographic archive, go to www.heritagetrust.wwwinter.co.uk. The trust offers volunteering opportunities for those who want to get more thoroughly involved.

# 110 Wright of Derby

*Artistic enlightenment*

One of the most original and versatile artists of his day, Joseph Wright (1734–1797) was born and raised in Derby at a time when the town was a clamour of literary and scientific ideas. In the 1780s, these ideas coalesced at meetings of the Derby Philosophical Society, whose Enlightenment preoccupations included a belief that the pursuit of scientific knowledge would inevitably improve the human condition.

Wright was an active member of the Society and shared its enthusiasms. And, indeed, living in Derby, a burgeoning industrial town, seems to have suited him very well: at one time or another, Wright lived in London, Bath and Italy, but he always returned to Derby and it is, therefore, singularly appropriate that the Derby Museum and Art Gallery holds a delightful and impressively large collection of his works.

In the Joseph Wright Gallery, you can see how the artist first established himself as a portraitist with acutely observed paintings of the gentry mingled with self-portraits of a sharp, almost ironic sensitivity. Later, in the 1760s, Wright's artistic interests took a turn as he became increasingly fascinated by light, especially moon and candlelight. Sometimes the results could be fairly prosaic – as in some of his Mount Vesuvius paintings – but when Wright came to the scientific world the results were nothing short of startling, with the artist able to catch – almost bottle – the fervent spirit of the Enlightenment. A prime example, and one of Wright's most rhapsodic paintings, is *A Philosopher Giving That Lecture on the Orrery, in Which a Lamp is Put in Place of the Sun*. This depicts a red-gowned tutor giving a lecture on astronomy to an enraptured audience by means of a clockwork model of the solar system called an orrery. First exhibited in 1766, the painting secured Wright's reputation as one of England's finest artists.

**Address** Derby Museum & Art Gallery, The Strand, Derby, DE1 1BS, +44 (0)1332 641901, www.derbymuseums.org | **Getting there** A 12-minute walk from Derby bus station | **Hours** Tue–Sat 10am–5pm, Sun noon–4pm | **Tip** If you enjoy Wright's paintings, be sure to pop into Derby Museum's Joseph Wright Study Room, which holds a collection of Wright's drawings, as well as prints, letters and other archive material.

# 111 Ye Olde Dolphin Inne

*Stand and deliver!*

Once hemmed in by ramshackle buildings, the attractive half-timbered façade of Ye Olde Dolphin Inne now has space of its own, just a few yards from the Cathedral. This is Derby's oldest surviving pub, but although parts of the building date back to the middle of the 16th century, it has been restored and modified on several occasions, most notably in the 1950s. A handsome, big-eyed dolphin now decorates the exterior, the latest in a series of ornamental dolphins that seem to date right back, reflecting the animal's importance as a Christian symbol – dolphins were credited with carrying the deceased to the afterlife, as they were in pagan times before.

Given the age of the pub, it's no surprise that all sorts of ghoulish legends have attached themselves to the place, especially as the rear section was originally a doctor's house, where the owner seems to have dissected the bodies of executed criminals willy-nilly. Among the legends still swirling around, choose from the Grey Lady who haunts the bar, the sad boy on the stairs, or the screaming girl who lives in the cellar. Apparitions aside, Ye Olde Dolphin Inne has had a bumpy history, no more so than when it was a stopping-off point for the highwaymen who roamed Derbyshire in the late 17th and early 18th centuries. The ancient highway linking Derby and Chesterfield was their prime hunting ground: the robbers sized up their victims in Derby and then picked them off as they straggled across the Peaks, all at a time when there were no reliable maps.

Local legend asserts that Dick Turpin (1705–1739), the most famous highwayman of them all, was a regular visitor to Ye Olde Dolphin Inne on account of a woman who lived here. This may or may not be true, but there again not many of his fellow drinkers were ever likely to challenge Turpin, a real hard case, who was well-known for his ferocious temper.

**Address** 5 Queen Street, Derby, DE1 3DL, +44 (0)1332 389568, www.yeoldedolphin.co.uk | **Getting there** A 10-minute walk from Derby bus station | **Hours** Sun–Thu noon–11pm, Fri & Sat noon–midnight, but these can change so check the website | **Tip** It's the shortest of walks from Ye Olde Dolphin to Silk Mill Park, a welcome chunk of greenery that stretches down to the River Derwent.

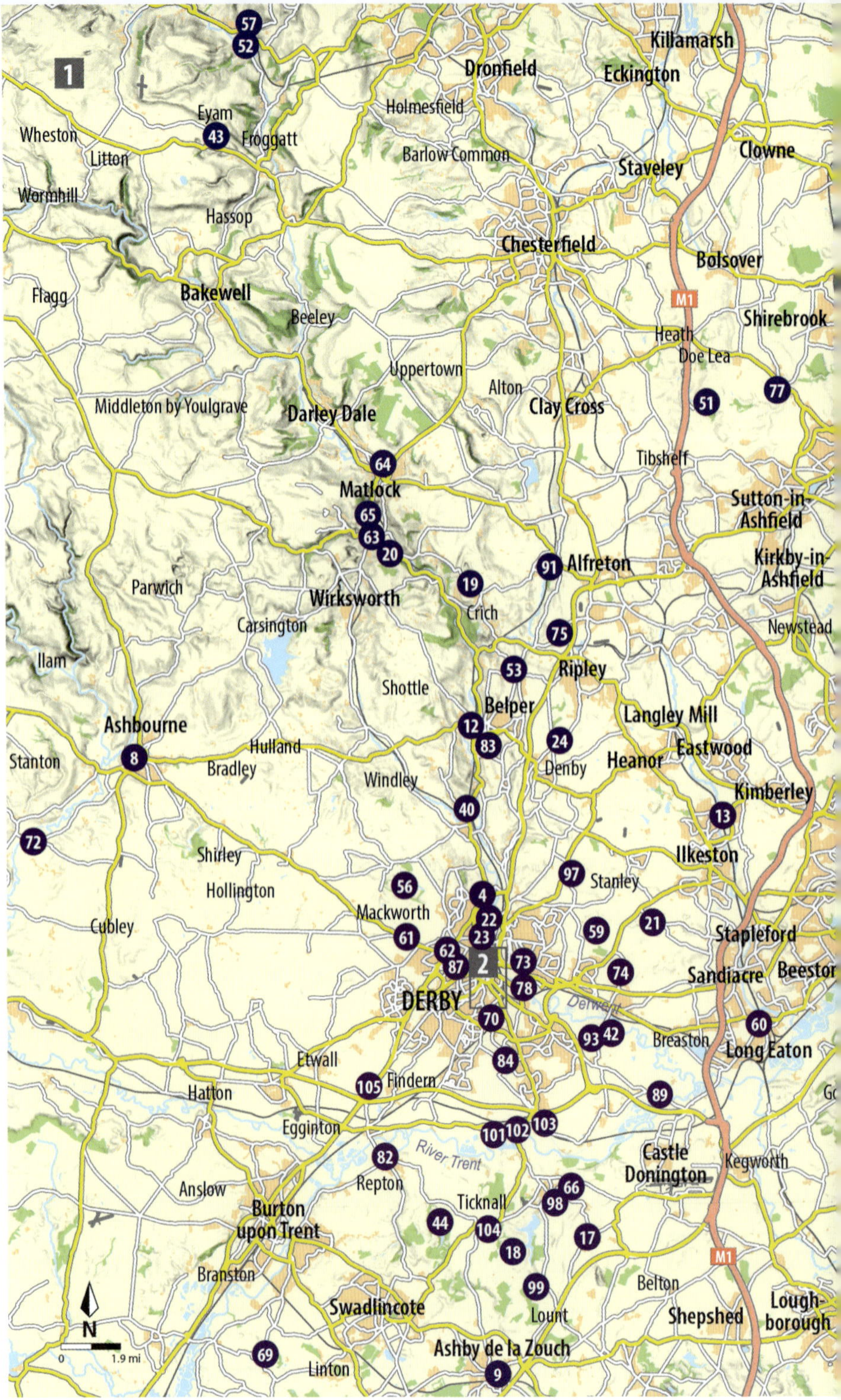

1
2
Killamarsh
Dronfield
Eckington
Eyam
Holmesfield
Wheston
Froggatt
Litton
Barlow Common
Clowne
Staveley
Wormhill
Hassop
Chesterfield
Bolsover
M1
Flagg
Bakewell
Beeley
Shirebrook
Heath
Doe Lea
Uppertown
Alton
Middleton by Youlgrave
Darley Dale
Clay Cross
Tibshelf
Matlock
Sutton-in-Ashfield
Kirkby-in-Ashfield
Alfreton
Parwich
Wirksworth
Crich
Carsington
Newstead
Ilam
Ripley
Shottle
Belper
Langley Mill
Ashbourne
Eastwood
Hulland
Stanton
Heanor
Denby
Bradley
Windley
Kimberley
Shirley
Ilkeston
Stanley
Hollington
Mackworth
Cubley
Stapleford
Sandiacre
Beeston
DERBY
Derwent
Breaston
Long Eaton
Etwall
Findern
Hatton
Egginton
River Trent
Castle Donington
Kegworth
Anslow
Repton
Ticknall
Burton upon Trent
Branston
Belton
Swadlincote
Lount
Shepshed
Lough-borough
N
0
1.9 mi
Ashby de la Zouch
Linton
57
52
43
77
51
64
65
63
20
91
19
75
53
12
83
24
8
40
13
72
97
56
4
22
23
61
59
21
62
87
73
74
78
70
60
93
42
84
105
89
101
102
103
82
66
98
44
104
17
18
99
69
9

Little Chester
85
2
3
49
Duffield Road
Mansfield Road
Stores Road
Sir Frank Whittle Road
Cowley Street
Kedleston Road
West End
36
Saint Alkmund's Way
King Street
Bridge Street
Nottingham
The Pentagon
Friar Gate
Agard Street
Ford Street
Cathedral Quarter
Derwent Street
Eastgate Junction
Eastgate
76
47
46
106
Full Street
Darwin Place
Stafford Street
DERBY
Derwent
Morledge
Curzon Street
Uttoxeter New Road
Macklin Street
Saint Peters Quarter
Pride Parkway
Station Approach
Green Lane
Babington Lane
Castlefields
Traffic Street
5
Mercian Way
Castleward
80
Stockbrook Street
Abbey Street
Lara Croft Way
71
Railway Terrace
31
37
Midland Road
67
109
Boyer Street
London Road
55
Mill Hill Lane
86
Burton Road
New Normanton
Bateman Street
Whitaker Road
Saint Chads Road
Normanton Road
26
Rose Hill
6
Douglas Street
7
Osmaston Road
Stanhope Street
Pear Tree Road
33
Dairy House Road
N
0
170 yd
10
Upper Dale Road

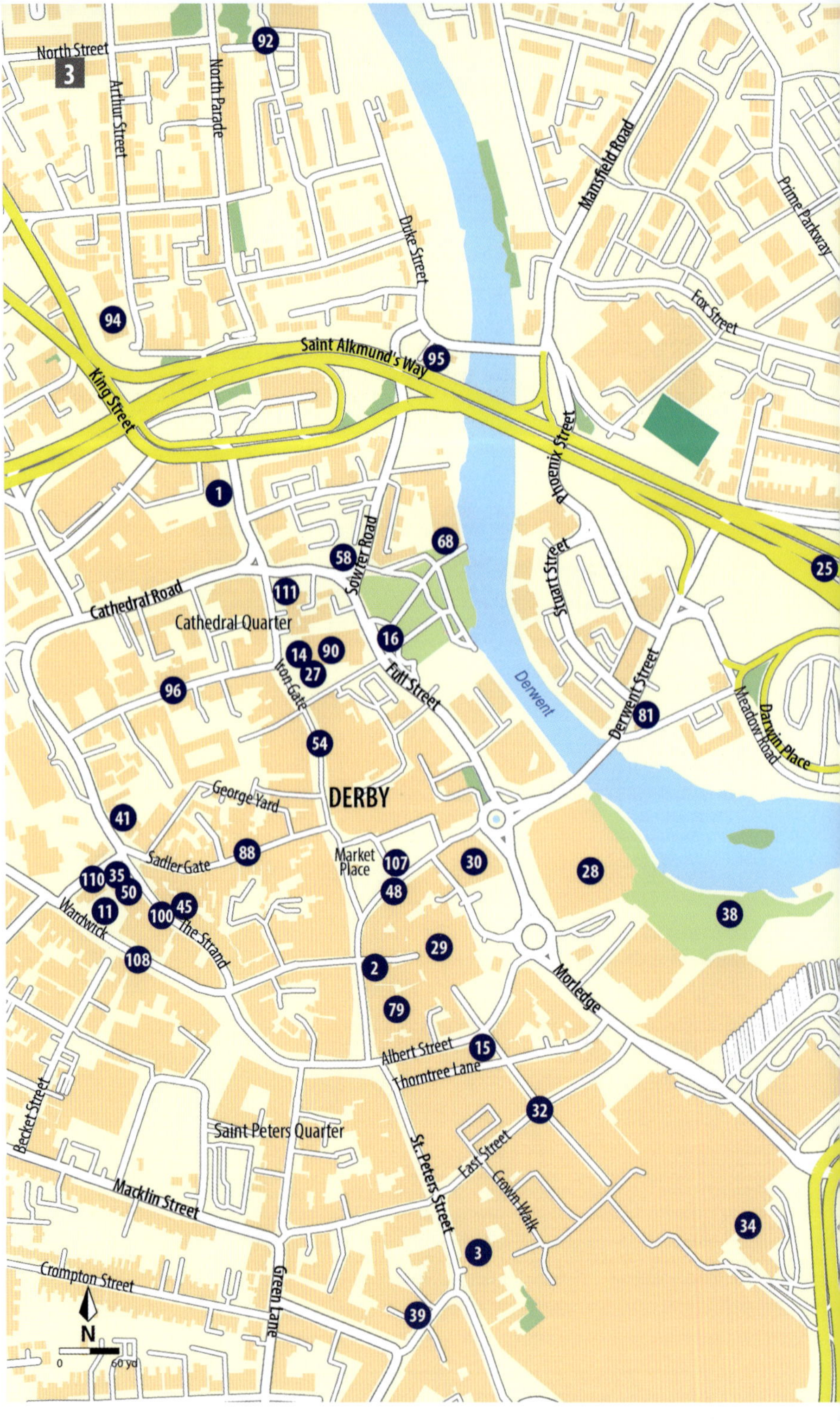
3
North Street
Arthur Street
North Parade
Duke Street
Mansfield Road
Prime Parkway
Fox Street
Saint Alkmund's Way
King Street
Phoenix Street
Sowter Road
Stuart Street
Cathedral Road
Cathedral Quarter
Iron Gate
Full Street
Derwent
Derwent Street
Meadow Road
Darwin Place
DERBY
George Yard
Sadler Gate
Market Place
Wardwick
The Strand
Morledge
Albert Street
Thorntree Lane
Becket Street
Saint Peters Quarter
East Street
Crown Walk
St. Peters Street
Macklin Street
Crompton Street
Green Lane
N
0
60 yd

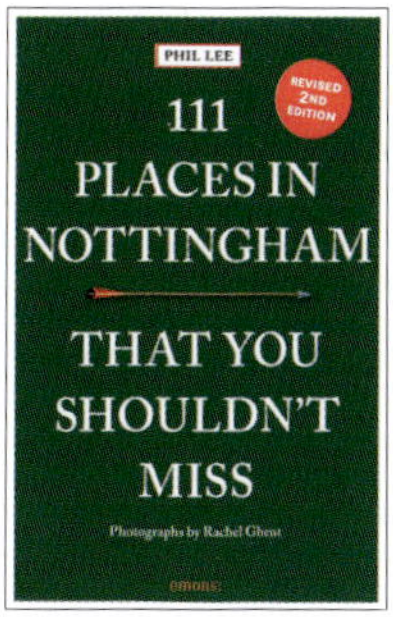


Phil Lee, Rachel Ghent
**111 Places in Nottingham That You Shouldn't Miss**
ISBN 978-3-7408-2261-3

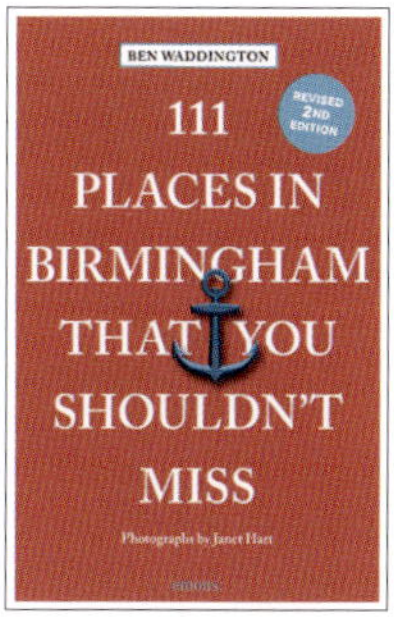


Ben Waddington, Janet Hart
**111 Places in Birmingham That You Shouldn't Miss**
ISBN 978-3-7408-2268-2

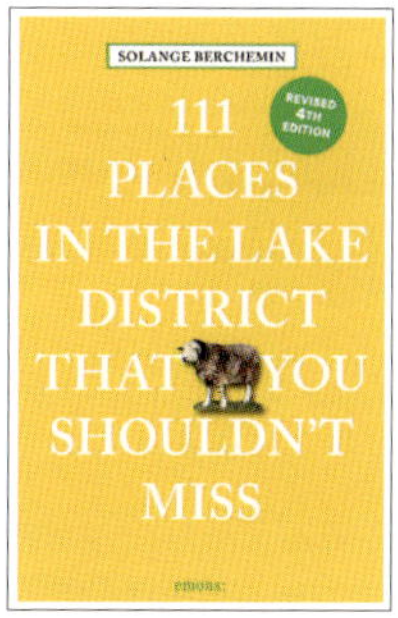


Solange Berchemin
**111 Places in the Lake District That You Shouldn't Miss**
ISBN 978-3-7408-2404-4

Ed Glinert, David Taylor
**111 Places in Oxford That You Shouldn't Miss**
ISBN 978-3-7408-1990-3

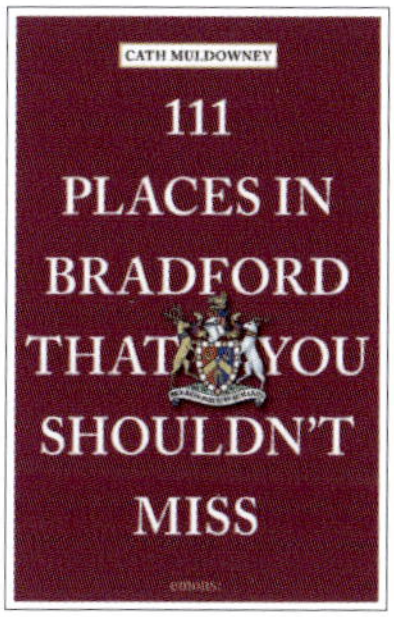


Cath Muldowney
**111 Places in Bradford That You Shouldn't Miss**
ISBN 978-3-7408-1427-4

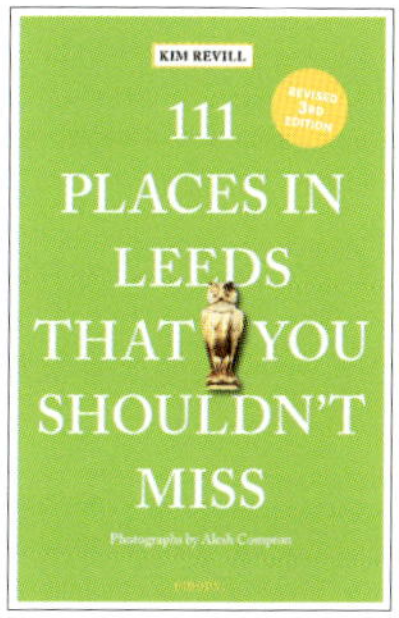


Kim Revill, Alesh Compton
**111 Places in Leeds That You Shouldn't Miss**
ISBN 978-3-7408-2059-6

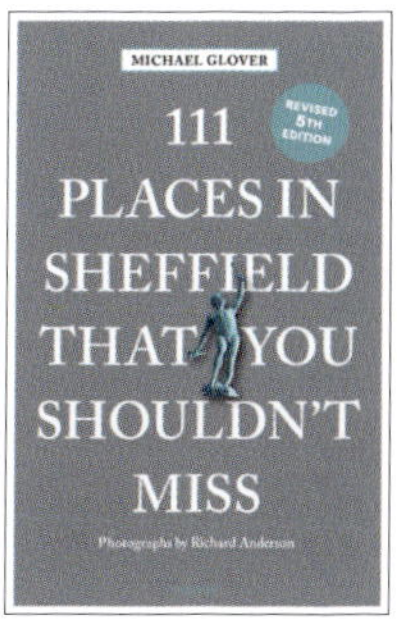


Michael Glover, Richard Anderson
**111 Places in Sheffield That You Shouldn't Miss**
ISBN 978-3-7408-2348-1

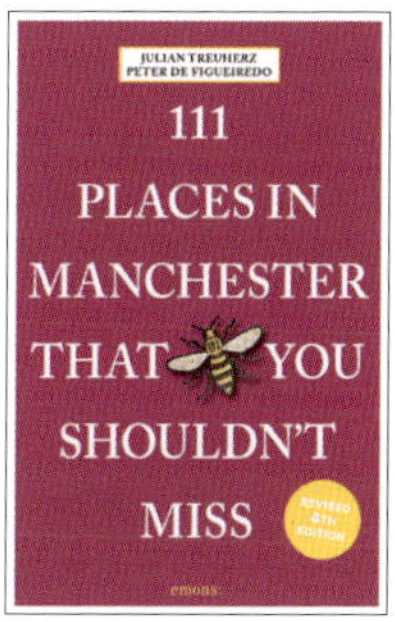


Julian Treuherz, Peter de Figueiredo
**111 Places in Manchester That You Shouldn't Miss**
ISBN 978-3-7408-2246-0

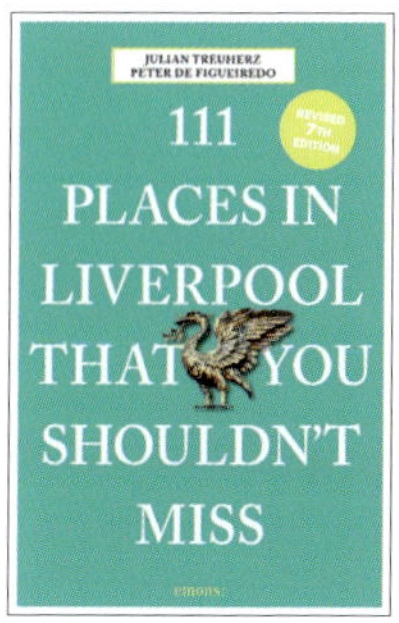


Julian Treuherz, Peter de Figueiredo
**111 Places in Liverpool That You Shouldn't Miss**
ISBN 978-3-7408-2515-7

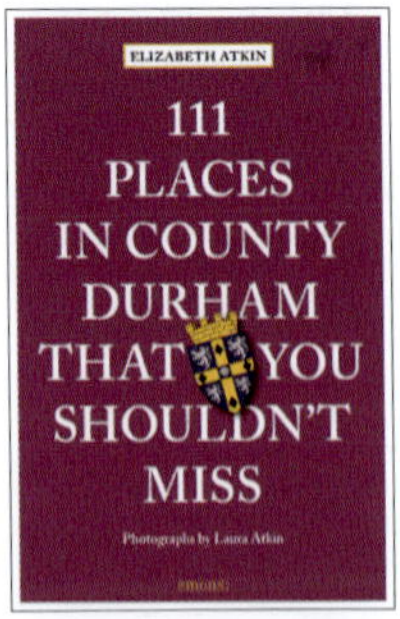


Elizabeth Atkin, Laura Atkin
**111 Places in County Durham That You Shouldn't Miss**
ISBN 978-3-7408-1426-7

David Taylor
**111 Places in Newcastle That You Shouldn't Miss**
ISBN 978-3-7408-1043-6

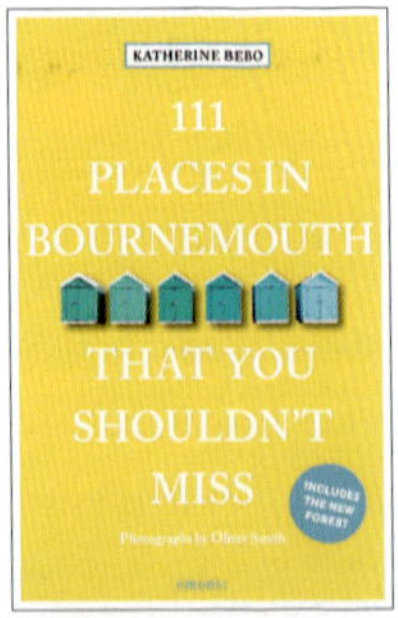


Katherine Bebo, Oliver Smith
**111 Places in Bournemouth That You Shouldn't Miss**
ISBN 978-3-7408-1166-2

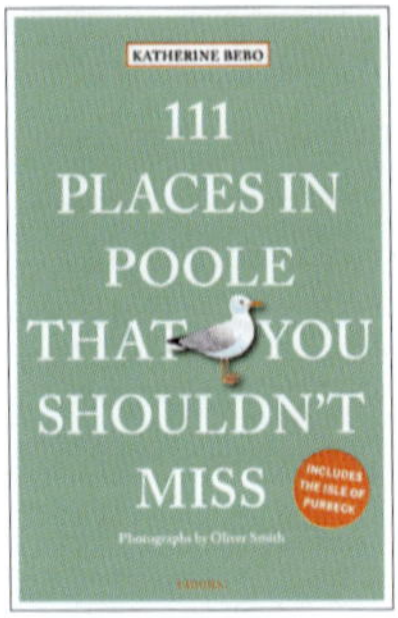


Katherine Bebo, Oliver Smith
**111 Places in Poole That You Shouldn't Miss**
ISBN 978-3-7408-0598-2

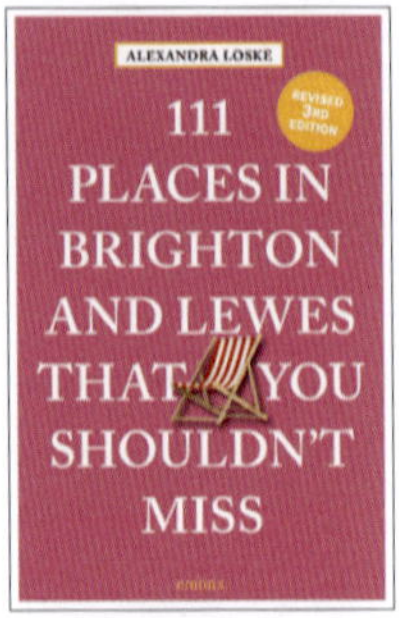


Alexandra Loske
**111 Places in Brighton and Lewes That You Shouldn't Miss**
ISBN 978-3-7408-1727-5

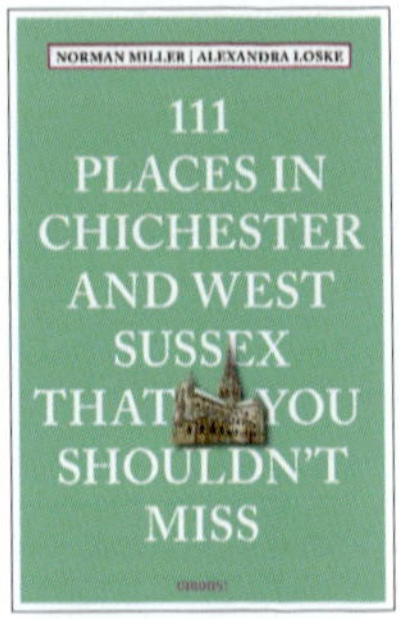


Norman Miller, Alexandra Loske
**111 Places in Chichester and West Sussex That You Shouldn't Miss**
ISBN 978-3-7408-1784-8

Catriona Neil, Adrian Spalding
**111 Places in Cornwall That You Shouldn't Miss**
ISBN 978-3-7408-1901-9

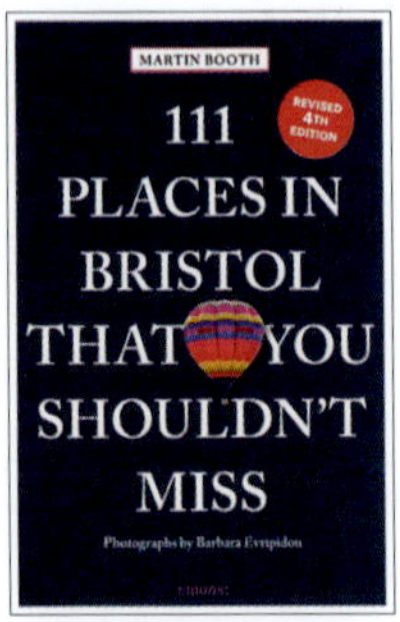


Martin Booth, Barbara Evripidou
**111 Places in Bristol That You Shouldn't Miss**
ISBN 978-3-7408-2001-5

Martin Booth, Barbara Evripidou
**111 Places for Kids in Bristol That You Shouldn't Miss**
ISBN 978-3-7408-1665-0

David Taylor
**111 Places in Northumberland That You Shouldn't Miss**
ISBN 978-3-7408-1792-3

Ed Glinert, David Taylor
**111 Places in Yorkshire That You Shouldn't Miss**
ISBN 978-3-7408-1167-9

Ed Glinert, Karin Tearle
**111 Places in Essex That You Shouldn't Miss**
ISBN 978-3-7408-1593-6

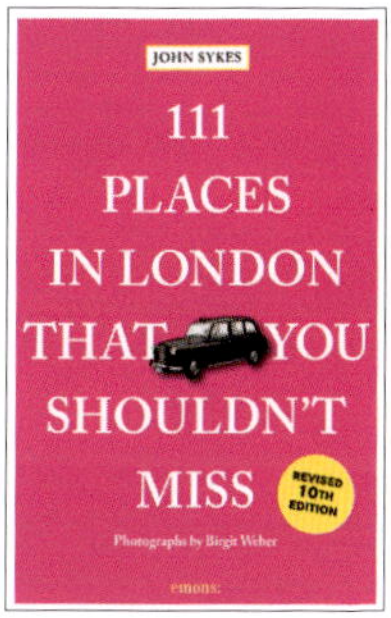


John Sykes, Birgit Weber
**111 Places in London That You Shouldn't Miss**
ISBN 978-3-7408-2379-5

Alicia Edwards
**111 Places for Kids in London That You Shouldn't Miss**
ISBN 978-3-7408-2196-8

Michael Glover, Benedict Flett
**111 Hidden Art Treasures in London That You Shouldn't Miss**
ISBN 978-3-7408-1576-9

Terry Philpot, Karin Tearle
**111 Literary Places in London That You Shouldn't Miss**
ISBN 978-3-7408-1954-5

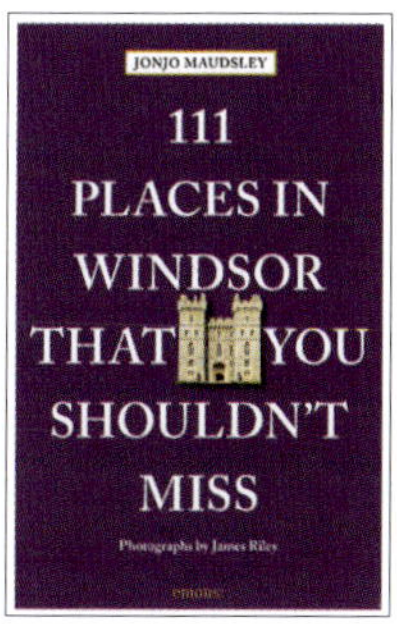


Jonjo Maudsley, James Riley
**111 Places in Windsor That You Shouldn't Miss**
ISBN 978-3-7408-2009-1

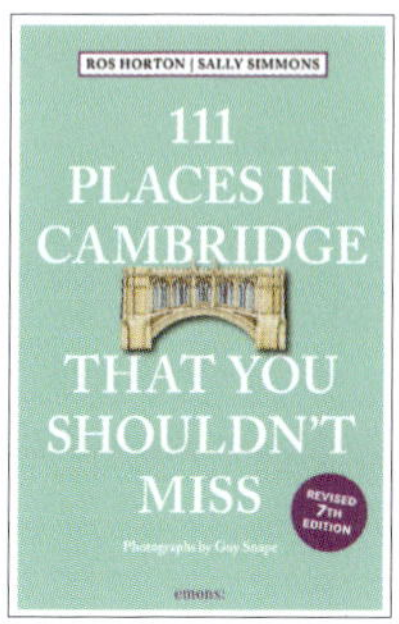


Rosalind Horton, Sally Simmons, Guy Snape
**111 Places in Cambridge That You Shouldn't Miss**
ISBN 978-3-7408-2376-4

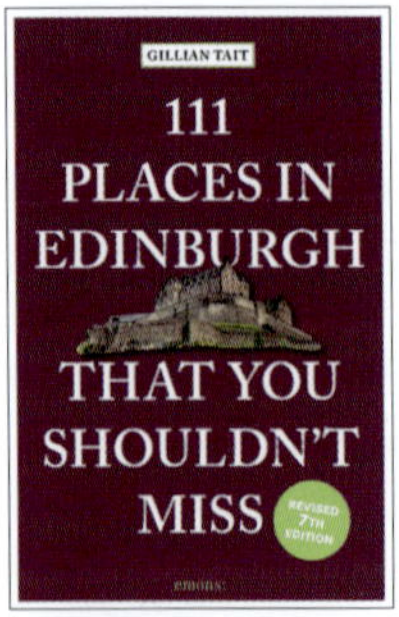


Gillian Tait
**111 Places in Edinburgh**
**That You Shouldn't Miss**
ISBN 978-3-7408-2575-1

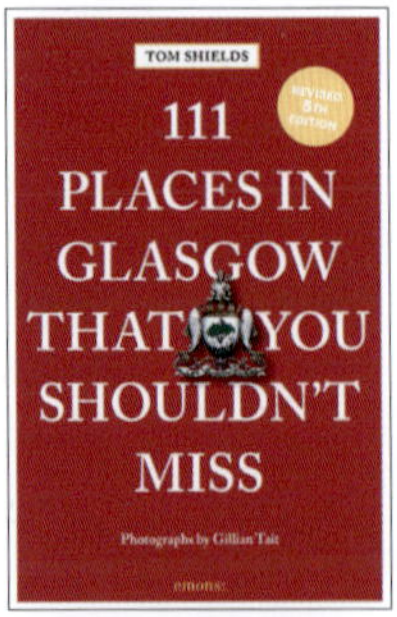


Tom Shields, Gillian Tait
**111 Places in Glasgow**
**That You Shouldn't Miss**
ISBN 978-3-7408-2237-8

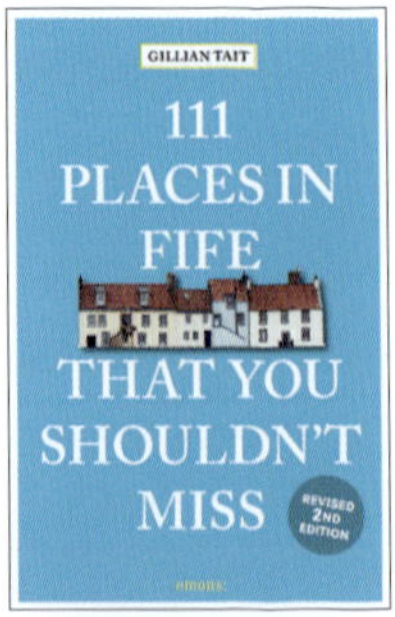


Gillian Tait
**111 Places in Fife**
**That You Shouldn't Miss**
ISBN 978-3-7408-0597-5

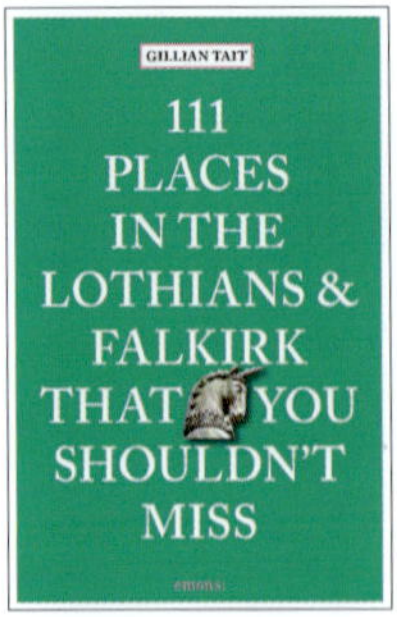


Gillian Tait
**111 Places**
**in the Lothians and Falkirk**
**That You Shouldn't Miss**
ISBN 978-3-7408-1569-1

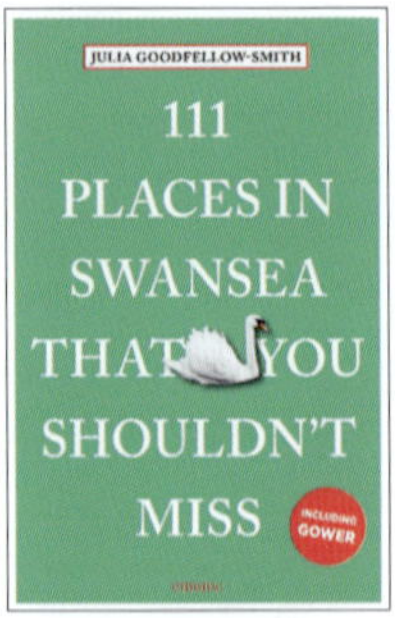


Julia Goodfellow-Smith
**111 Places in Swansea**
**That You Shouldn't Miss**
ISBN 978-3-7408-2065-7

Jo-Anne Elikann, Susan Lusk
**111 Places in New York**
**That You Must Not Miss**
ISBN 978-3-7408-2400-6

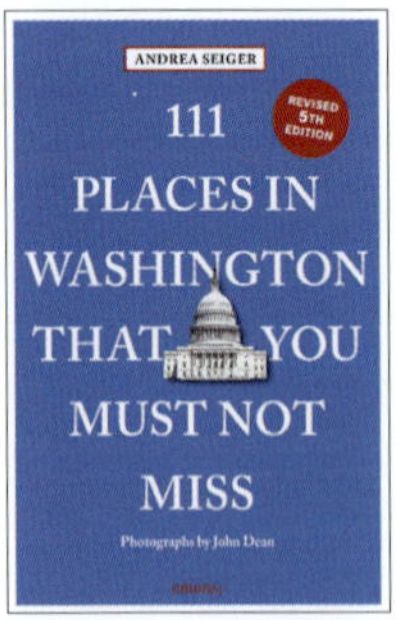


Andrea Seiger, John Dean
**111 Places in Washington**
**That You Must Not Miss**
ISBN 978-3-7408-2399-3

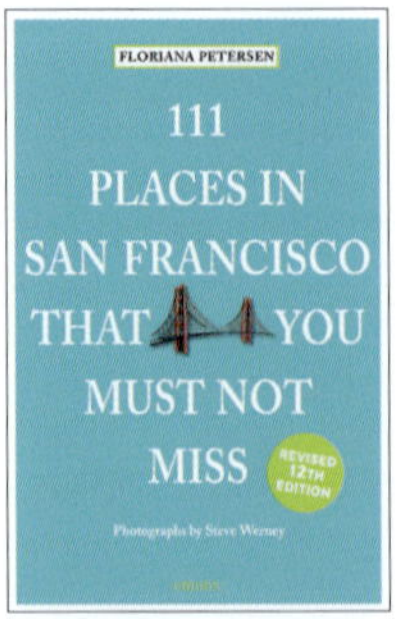


Floriana Petersen, Steve Werney
**111 Places in San Francisco**
**That You Must Not Miss**
ISBN 978-3-7408-2058-9

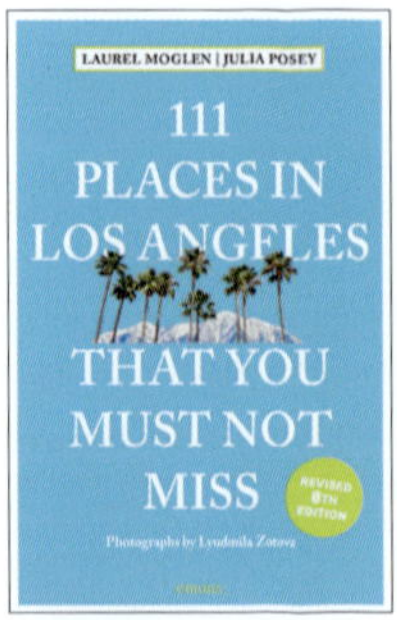


Laurel Moglen, Julia Posey,
Lyudmila Zotova
**111 Places in Los Angeles**
**That You Must Not Miss**
ISBN 978-3-7408-1889-0

# Acknowledgements

So many friends and acquaintances have chipped in with ideas for this book, I hardly know where to begin. But I do want to thank Rod Wood for his Derby tips; Chez Abrams for driving me round – she's a much better driver than I am, as is wall-of-death driver Ruth Rigby, who also helped me get around. Thanks also to Peter Smith for trips and tips; my brother David Lee for advice on Crich Tramway; John Scruton and Peter Collins of the Friends of Bennerley Viaduct; James Lawless of David Mellor Design; Roger Hatcher, and Anthony and Patricia Sharp of Heage Windmill; Heidi McKenzie and Iain Hayes of Derby Theatre; Gurpal Singh from the National Sikh Museum; Amanda Mundin from the Ritz, Belper; Andrew Orpe from St Batholomew's, Elvaston; Paul Burrows of the Royal School for the Deaf; Sheila Randall of St Matthew's, Morley; Mary Baker of Swarkestone Church; Dr Alex Rock, Director of Commercial Operations at Derby Museums Trust; Alison Buckley of Elvaston Castle & Gardens; and Susan Bookbinder.

Special thanks also to the helpful and refreshingly efficient Stella Birks and Michelle Booth from the Tourism Team of Derby City Council. A big thank you also to the photographer, Rachel Ghent, and her partner, Simon, who have been a source of many great tips and ideas. Last but not least, thanks to Laura Olk of Emons, the publisher, for all her patience and marshalling of the whole process, and to my excellent editor, Ros Horton, for all her hard work and attention to detail.

**Phil Lee** was born and raised in Nottingham and he just couldn't escape the clutches of his home city, returning after a spell as a merchant seaman in the Danish navy. He lives there still, very happily, and has carved out a varied career as a travel writer. One of his most recent books is *111 Places in Nottingham That You Shouldn't Miss*, published in 2024.

**Rachel Ghent** is originally from the North East, and studied photography in Newcastle before settling in Long Eaton nine years ago. Living between Nottingham and Derby, she splits her downtime between the two. She's a regular at the fabulous Museum of Making and is a fan of Derby's newly refurbished Market Hall. You'll often find her enjoying a pint of cask ale at her favourite boozers – The Alex and Smithfield.

The information in this book was accurate at the time of publication, but it can change at any time. Please confirm the details for the places you're planning to visit before you head out on your adventures.